CITY DEVELOPMENT

City Development

Studies in
Disintegration and Renewal

LEWIS MUMFORD

GREENWOOD PRESS, PUBLISHERS
WESTPORT, CONNECTICUT

Library of Congress Cataloging in Publication Data

Mumford, Lewis, 1895–
   City development.

    Reprint of the ed. published by Harcourt, Brace,
New York.
    1. Cities and towns. 2. Cities and towns—
Planning—1945–   3. Cities and towns—Planning—
London. 4. Cities and towns—Planning—Honolulu.
I. Title.
HT151.M77 1973   309.2'62   73-6212
ISBN 0-8371-6890-2

Copyright 1945, © 1973 by Lewis Mumford

Originally published in 1945
by Harcourt, Brace and Company, New York

Reprinted with the permission of Lewis Mumford

First Greenwood Reprinting 1973

Library of Congress Catalogue Card Number 73-6212

ISBN 0-8371-6890-2

Printed in the United States of America

In 1915—just thirty years ago—I first came across City Development; A Study of Parks, Gardens, and Culture Institutes, by Patrick Geddes, published in 1904. That book stirred one of the chief interests of my life. The essays I have chosen to group together here are the most representative selections of my work in the field of urbanism during the last quarter century. In a spirit of piety, I have given them the title of the book that originally stimulated them, now long out of print. All these essays of mine are inaccessible except the last two; the latter, however, now appear for the first time in the United States. Until I have the opportunity to bring out a revised edition of The Culture of Cities, the final two papers in the present volume must serve to show what revisions have taken place in my thinking about the planning and ordering of cities, as a result of the catastrophe that has been steadily engulfing our whole civilization.

L. M.

CONTENTS

CITY DEVELOPMENT

THE CITY

The City was written for the symposium on Civilization in the United States, edited by Harold Stearns: * *published in 1922. It was, I believe, the first historic analysis of its kind to be published in the United States; and both in its perceptions and its omissions it bears witness to the current state of thought. I was twenty-six when I wrote that essay, and still had much to learn, both about that large part of the history of my country which had hardly been touched by any of the historians, and about the development of cities themselves: yet I am not ashamed to publish it along with my maturer work, even though it tempt some unfriendly critic to remark how little I have learned since.*

Despite more than a generation of constructive effort toward the improvement of cities, led by Frederick Law Olmsted, the elder, one of the great artists of the nineteenth century, comparatively little work had then been done in the detailed history of American city building or in a sociological analysis of the processes themselves. The advance of the Chicago school of urban sociologists had been somewhat tangential, and such works as Carl Bridenbaugh's Cities in the Wilderness, or John Coolidge's Mill and Mansion, still lay in the future. For more than a generation, we had indeed had among us the most brilliant and penetrating critic of architecture America has yet produced, Montgomery Schuyler, one

* Copyright 1922 by Harcourt, Brace and Company, Inc.

3

of the first to make a sound critical appraisal of the Roeblings, Richardson, Adler and Sullivan; but good though Schuyler was, his field was the individual building, not the corporate organization and plan.

There are many points in my essay that would now have to be amplified; and certain uninformed judgments remain, like that on Richardson, which I myself have since corrected in various other places; still I leave it as it stands, because its errors have but little capacity for mischief. In my contribution to the Survey Graphic's Regional Planning Number, May 1925, I made a somewhat different analysis of our urban growth, dividing it into an initial period of settlement, with three subsequent migrations, leading to the possibility of a fourth migration which would be in the nature of a wholesale resettlement of the country.

Even before 1922 I had left behind the notion that metropolitanism was a mark of progress or a conclusive phase in the development of cities: hence my unsparing criticism of the Regional Plan for New York, sponsored by the Russell Sage Foundation, whose naïve premises I criticized at the very beginning of their work and whose final report I analyzed in some detail in the New Republic in 1932. The assumptions about continued population growth and urban concentration which the Russell Sage planners regarded as so eminently sensible and unchallengeable have now been proved worthless, for the very civilization that supported these beliefs is, in many areas, in an advanced stage of disintegration.

Meanwhile these false premises did great harm by distracting attention from the real problems that confronted our cities and by failing to work out any strategy for dealing with these problems. As so often has happened during the last quarter century, the self-styled practical men turned out to be the weak irresponsible dreamers, afraid to face unpleasant

*facts, while those of us who were called dreamers have, per-
haps, some little right to be accepted—at least belatedly—as
practical men. By now history has caught up with our most
dire prophecies. That is at once the justification of our thinking and the proof of its tragic failure to influence our contemporaries.*

1. PROVINCIAL AND COMMERCIAL ERAS

Around us, in the city, each epoch in America has been
concentrated and crystallized. In building our cities we deflowered a wilderness. Today more than one-half the population of the United States lives in an environment which
the jerry-builder, the real estate speculator, the paving con-
tractor, and the industrialist have largely created. Have we
begotten a civilization? That is a question which a survey
of the American city will help us to answer.

If American history is viewed from the standpoint of the
student of cities, it divides itself roughly into three parts.
The first was a provincial period, which lasted from the
foundation of Manhattan down to the opening up of ocean
commerce after the War of 1812. This was followed by a
commercial period, which began with the cutting of canals
and ended with the extension of the railroad system across
the continent, and an industrial period, that gathered force
on the Atlantic seaboard in the thirties and is still the dominant economic phase of our civilization. These periods must
not be looked upon as strictly successive or exclusive: the
names merely express in a crude way the main aspect of each
era. It is possible to telescope the story of America's colonial
expansion and industrial exploitation by following the ma-

terial growth and the cultural impoverishment of the American city during its transformations.

The momentum of the provincial city lasted well on to the Civil War. The economic basis of this period was agriculture and petty trade: its civic expression was, typically, the small New England town, with a central common around which were grouped a church—appropriately called a meeting house—a school, and perhaps a town hall. Its main street would be lined with tall suave elms and bordered by reticent white houses of much the same design as those that dotted the countryside. In the growing towns of the seaboard this culture was overthrown, before it had a chance to express itself adequately in either institutions or men, and it bloomed rather tardily, therefore, in the little towns of Concord and Cambridge, between 1820 and the Civil War. We know it today through a largely anonymous architecture, and through a literature created by the school of writers that bears the name of the chief city. Unfortunately for the further development of what we might call the Concord culture, the agricultural basis of this civilization shifted to the wheat-growing West; and therewith channels of trade were diverted from Boston to ports that tapped a richer, more imperial hinterland. What remained of the provincial town in New England was a mummy-case.

The civilization of the New England town spent itself in the settlement of the Ohio Valley and the great tracts beyond. None of the new centers had, as provincial towns, any fresh contribution to make. It had taken the culture of New England more than three centuries before it had borne its Concord fruit, and the story of the Western movement is somehow summed up in the legend of Johnny Appleseed, who planted dry apple seeds, instead of grafts from the living tree, and hedged the roads he traveled with wild apples, harsh and

puny and inedible. Cincinnati and Pittsburgh jumped from
a frustrate provincialism into the midst of the machine era;
and so for a long time they remained destitute of the institutions that are necessary to carry on the processes of
civilization.

West of the Alleghanies, the common, with its church and
school, was not destined to dominate the urban landscape: the
railroad station and the commercial hotel had come to take
their place. This was indeed the universal mark of the new
industrialism, as obvious in nineteenth-century Oxford as in
Hoboken. The pioneer American city, however, had none of
the cultural institutions that had been accumulated in Europe
during the great outbursts of the Middle Age and the Renaissance, and as a result its destitution was naked and apparent.
It is true that every town which was developed mainly during
the nineteenth century—Manchester as well as Milwaukee—
suffered from the absence of civic institutes. The peculiarity
of the New World was that the facilities for borrowing from
the older centers were considerably more limited. London
could export Madox Brown to Manchester to do the murals
in the Town Hall: New York had still to create its schools
of art before it had any Madox Browns that could be
exported.

With the beginning of the nineteenth-century market centers
which had at first tapped only their immediate region began
to reach further back into the hinterland, and to stretch outward, not merely for freights but for immigrants, across the
ocean. The silly game of counting heads became the fashion,
and in the literature of the thirties one discovers that every
commercial city had its statistical lawyer who was bold
enough to predict its leadership in "population and wealth"
before the century was out. The chief boast of the American
city was its prospective size.

Now the New England town was a genuine community. In so far as the New England community had a common social and political and religious life, the town expressed it. The city which was representative of the second period, on the other hand, was in origin a trading fort, and the supreme occupation of its founders was with the goods life rather than the good life. New York, Pittsburgh, Chicago, and St. Louis have this common basis. They were not composed of corporate organizations on the march, as it were, towards a New Jerusalem: they were simply a rabble of individuals "on the make." With such a tradition to give it momentum it is small wonder that the adventurousness of the commercial period was exhausted on the fortuities and temptations of trade. A state of intellectual anesthesia prevailed. One has only to compare Cist's Cincinnati Miscellany with Emerson's Dial to see at what a low level the towns of the Middle West were carrying on.

Since there was neither fellowship nor social stability nor security in the scramble of the inchoate commercial city, it remained for a particular institution to devote itself to the gospel of the "glad hand." Thus an historian of Pittsburgh records the foundation of a Masonic lodge as early as 1785, shortly after the building of the church, and in every American city, small or big, Odd Fellows, Mystic Shriners, Woodmen, Elks, Knights of Columbus, and other orders without number in the course of time found for themselves a prominent place. (Their feminine counterparts were the D.A.R. and the W.C.T.U., their juniors, the college Greek letter fraternities.) Whereas one will search American cities in vain for the labor temples one discovers today in Europe from Belgium to Italy, one finds that the fraternal lodge generally occupies a site of dignity and importance. There were doubtless many excellent reasons for the strange proliferation of professional fraternity in the American city, but perhaps the strongest reason was the absence of any other kind of fraternity. The social center and the community center, which in a singularly hard and consciously beatific way have sought to organize fellowship and mutual aid on different terms, are products of the last decade.

Perhaps the only other civic institution of importance that the commercial towns fostered was the lyceum: forerunner of the elephantine Chautauqua. The lyceum lecture, however, was taken as a soporific rather than a stimulant, and if it aroused any appetite for art, philosophy, or science there was nothing in the environment of the commercial city that could satisfy it. Just as church going became a substitute for religion, so automatic lyceum attendance became a substitute for thought. These were the prayer wheels of a preoccupied commercialism.

The contrast between the provincial and the commercial city in America was well summed up in their plans. Consider the differences between Cambridge and New York. Up to the beginning of the nineteenth century New York, at the tip of Manhattan Island, had the same diffident, rambling town plan that characterizes Cambridge. In this old type of city layout the streets lead nowhere, except to the buildings that give onto them: outside the main roads the provisions for traffic are so inadequate as to seem almost a provision against traffic. Quiet streets, a pleasant aspect, ample domestic facilities were the desiderata of the provincial town; traffic, realty speculation, and expansion were those of the newer era. This became evident as soon as the Empire City started to realize its "manifest destiny" by laying down, in 1811, a plan for its future development.

New York's city plan commissioners went about their work with a scarcely concealed purpose to increase traffic and raise realty values. The amenities of city life counted for little in their scheme of things: debating "whether they should confine themselves to rectilinear and rectangular streets, or whether they should adopt some of those supposed improvements, by circles, ovals, and stars," they decided, on grounds of economy, against any departure from the gridiron design. It was under the same stimulus that these admirable philistines had the complacency to plan the city's development up to 155th Street. Here we are concerned, however, with the results of the rectangular plan rather than with the motives that lay behind its adoption throughout the country.

The principal effect of the gridiron plan is that every street becomes a thoroughfare, and that every thoroughfare is potentially a commercial street. The tendency towards movement in such a city vastly outweighs the tendency towards settlement. As a result of progressive shifts in population, due to the changes to which commercial competition subjects the use of land, the main institutions of the city, instead of cohering naturally—as the museums, galleries, theaters, clubs, and public offices group themselves in the heart of Westminster—are dispersed in every direction. Neither Columbia College, New York University, the Astor Library, nor the National Academy of Design—to seize but a few examples—is on its original site. Yet had Columbia remained at Fiftieth Street it might have had some effective working relation with the great storehouse of books that now occupies part of Bryant Park at Forty-second Street; or, alternatively, had the Astor Library remained on its old site it might have had some connection with New York University—had that institution not in turn moved!

What was called the growth of the commercial city was really a manifestation of the absence of design in the grid-

iron plan. The rectangular parceling of ground promoted
speculation in land-units and the ready interchange of real
property: it had no relation whatever to the essential purposes for which a city exists. It is not a little significant that
Chicago, Cincinnati, and St. Louis, each of which had space
set aside for public purposes in their original plans, had
given up these civic holdings to the realty gambler before
half of the nineteenth century was over. The common was
not the center of a well-rounded community life, as in New
England, but the center of land-speculation—which was at
once the business, the recreation, and the religion of the
commercial city. Under the influence of New York the Scad-
ders, whom Martin Chuzzlewit encountered, were laying
down their New Edens throughout the country.

2. BROADWAY AS SYMBOL

It was during the commercial period that the evolution of
the Promenade, such as existed in New York at Battery Park,
took place. The new promenade was no longer a park but a
shop-lined thoroughfare, Broadway. Shopping became for
the more domesticated half of the community an exciting,
bewildering amusement; and out of a combination of Yankee
"notions," Barnumlike advertisement, and magisterial organization arose that *omnium gatherum* of commerce, the department store. It is scarcely possible to exaggerate the part
that Broadway—I use the term generically—has played in
the American town. It is not merely the Agora but the
Acropolis. When the factory whistle closes the week, and the
factory hands of Camden, or Pittsburgh, or Bridgeport pour
out of the buildings and stockades in which they spend the
more exhausting half of their lives, it is through Broadway
that the greater part of their repressions seek an outlet. Both
the name and the institution extend across the continent from

New York to Los Angeles. Up and down these second-hand Broadways, from one in the afternoon until past ten at night, drifts a more or less aimless mass of human beings, bent upon extracting such joy as is possible from the sights in the windows, the contacts with other human beings, the occasional or systematic flirtations, and the risks and adventures of purchase.

In the early development of Broadway the amusements were adventitious. Even at present, in spite of the ubiquitous movie, the crowded street itself, at least in the smaller communities, is the main source of entertainment. Now, under normal conditions, for a great part of the population in a factory town one of the chief instincts to be repressed is that of acquisition (collection). It is not merely that the average factory worker cannot afford the luxuries of life: the worst is that he must think twice before purchasing the necessities. Out of this situation one of Broadway's happiest achievements has arisen: the five and ten cent store. In the five and ten cent store it is possible for the circumscribed factory operative to obtain the illusion of unmoderated expenditure—and even extravagance—without actually inflicting any irreparable rent in his purse. Broadway is thus, in more than one sense, the great compensatory device of the American city. The dazzle of white lights, the color of electric signs, the alabaster architecture of the moving-picture palaces, the esthetic appeals of the shop windows—these stand for elements that are left out of the drab perspectives of the industrial city. People who do not know how to spend their time must take what satisfaction they can in spending their money. That is why, although the five and ten cent store itself is perhaps mainly an institution for the proletariat, the habits and dispositions it encourages are universal. The chief amusement of Atlantic City, that opulent hostelry-annex of

New York and Philadelphia, lies not in the beach and the ocean but in the shops which line the interminable Broadway known as the Boardwalk.

Broadway, in sum, is the façade of the American city: a false front. The highest achievements of our material civilization—and at their best our hotels, our department stores, and our Woolworth towers are achievements—count as so many symptoms of its spiritual failure. In order to cover up the vacancy of getting and spending in our cities, we have invented a thousand fresh devices for getting and spending. As a consequence our life is externalized. The principal institutions of the American city are merely distractions that take our eyes off the environment, instead of instruments which would help us to mold it creatively a little nearer to humane hopes and desires.

3. CONSEQUENCES OF INDUSTRIALISM

The birth of industrialism in America is announced in the opening of the Crystal Palace in Bryant Park, Manhattan, in 1853. Between the Crystal Palace Exhibition and the Chicago World's Fair in 1892 lies a period whose defects were partly accentuated by the exhaustion that followed the Civil War. The debasement of the American city during this period can be read in almost every building that was erected. The influence of colonial architecture had waned to extinction during the first half of the century. There followed a period of eclectic experiment, in which all sorts of Egyptian, Byzantine, Gothic, and Arabesque ineptitudes were committed—a period whose absurdities we have only in recent years begun to escape. The domestic style, as the century progressed, became more limited. Little touches about the doors, moldings, fanlights, and balustrades disappeared, and finally craftsmanship went out of style altogether and a pretentious

architectural puffery took its place. The "era of good feeling" was an era of bad taste.

Pittsburgh, St. Louis, and Chicago give perhaps the most
naked revelation of the industrial city's characteristics.
There were two institutions that set their mark upon the early
part of this period. One of them was the Mechanic's Hall.
This was usually a building of red brick, structural iron, and
glass, whose unique hideousness marks it as a typical product
of the age of coal-industrialism, to be put alongside the
"smoke-halls" of the railroad termini. The other institution
was the German beer-garden—the one bright spot on the edge
of an urban landscape that was steadily becoming more
dingy, more dull, and more depressing. The cities that came
to life in this period had scarcely any other civic apparatus
to boast of. Conceive of Pittsburgh without Schenley Park,
without the Carnegie Institute, without the Library or the
Museum or the Concert Hall, and without the institutions
that have grown up during the last generation around its
sub-Acropolis—and one has a picture of Progress and Poverty that Henry George might have drawn on for illustration. The industrial city did not represent the creative values
in civilization: it stood for a new form of human barbarism.
In the coal towns of Pennsylvania, the steel towns of the
Ohio and its tributaries, and the factory towns of Long Island
Sound and Narragansett Bay was an environment much more
harsh, antagonistic, and brutal than anything the pioneers
had encountered. Even the fake exhilaration of the commercial city was lacking.

The reaction against the industrial city was expressed in
various ways. The defect of these reactions was that they
were formulated in terms of an escape from the environment
rather than in a reconstruction of it. Symptomatic of this
escape, along one particular alley, was the architecture of

Richardson, and of his apprentices, McKim and White. No one who has an eye for the fine incidence of beautiful architecture can avoid a shock at discovering a monumental Romanesque building at the foot of Pittsburgh's dingy "Hump," or the hardly less monstrous beauty of Trinity Church, Boston, as one approaches it from a waste of railroad yards that lie on one side of it. It was no accident, one is inclined to believe, that Richardson should have returned to the Romanesque only a little time before Henry Adams was exploring Mont St. Michel and Chartres. Both men were searching for a specific against the fever of industrialism, and architects like Richardson were taking to archaic beauty as a man who was vaguely ill might have recourse to quinine, in the hope that his disease had sufficient similarity to malaria to be cured by it.

The truth is that the doses of exotic architecture which Richardson and his school sought to inject into the American city were anodynes rather than specifics. The Latin Renaissance models of McKim and White—the Boston Public Library and Madison Square Garden, for example—were perhaps a little better suited to the concrete demands of the new age; but they were still a long way from that perfect congruence with contemporary habits and modes of thought which was recorded in buildings like Independence Hall. Almost down to the last decade the best buildings of the industrial period have been anonymous, and scarcely ever recognized for their beauty. A grain elevator here, a warehouse there, an office building, a garage—there has been the promise of a stripped, athletic, classical style of architecture in these buildings which shall embody all that is good in the Machine Age: its precision, its cleanliness, its hard illuminations, its unflinching logic. Dickens once poked fun at the architecture of Coketown because its infirmary looked like its jail and its jail like its town hall. But the joke had a sting to it only because these buildings were all plaintively destitute of esthetic inspiration. In a place and an age that had achieved a well-rounded and balanced culture, we should expect to find the same spirit expressed in the simplest cottage and the grandest public building. So we find it, for instance, in the humble market towns of the Middle Age: there is not one type of architecture for fifteenth-century Shaftesbury and another for London; neither is there one style for public London and quite another for domestic London. Our architects in America have only just begun to cease regarding the Gothic style as especially fit for churches and schools, whilst they favor the Roman mode for courts, and the Byzantine, perhaps, for offices. Even the unique beauty of the Bush Terminal Tower is compromised by an antiquely "stylized" interior.*

With the beginning of the second decade of this century there is some evidence of an attempt to make a genuine culture out of industrialism—instead of attempting to escape from industrialism into a culture which, though doubtless genuine enough, has the misfortune to be dead. The schoolhouses in Gary, Indiana, have some of the better qualities of a Gary steel plant. That symptom is all to the good. It points perhaps to a time when the Gary steel plant may have some of the educational virtues of a Gary school. One of the things that has made the industrial age a horror in America is the notion that there is something shameful in its manifestations. The idea that nobody would ever go near an industrial plant except under stress of starvation is in part responsible for the heaps of rubbish and rusty metal, for

---

* This paragraph—like the article on Machinery and the Modern Style I published in The New Republic in 1921—antedated the lucubrations of Le Corbusier on the same subject.

the general disorder and vileness, that still characterize
broad acres of our factory districts. There is nothing short
of the Alkali Desert that compares with the desolateness of
the common American industrial town. These qualities are
indicative of the fact that we have centered attention not
upon the process but upon the return; not upon the task but
the emoluments; not upon what we can get out of our work
but upon what we can achieve when we get away from our
work. Our industrialism has been in the grip of business,
and our industrial cities, and their institutions, have exhibited a major preoccupation with business. The coercive
repression of an impersonal, mechanical technique was com-
pensated by the pervasive will-to-power—or at least will-to-
comfort—of commercialism.

We have shirked the problem of trying to live well in a
régime that is devoted to the production of T-beams and
toothbrushes and T.N.T. As a result, we have failed to react
creatively upon the environment with anything like the inspiration that one might have found in a group of medieval
peasants building a cathedral. The urban worker escapes
the mechanical routine of his daily job only to find an equally
mechanical substitute for life and growth and experience in
his amusements. The Gay White Way with its stupendous
blaze of lights, and Coney Island, with its fear-stimulating
roller coasters and chute-the-chutes, are characteristic by-
products of an age that has renounced the task of actively
humanizing the machine, and of creating an environment in
which all the fruitful impulses of the community may be
expressed. The movies, the White Ways, and the Coney
Islands, which almost every American city boasts in some
form or other, are means of giving jaded and throttled people
the sensations of living without the direct experience of life
—a sort of spiritual masturbation. In short, we have had

the alternative of humanizing the industrial city or de-humanizing the population. So far we have de-humanized the population.

4. EXODUS TO SUBURBIA

The external reactions against the industrial city came to a head in the World's Fair at Chicago. In that strange and giddy mixture of Parnassus and Coney Island was born a new conception of the city—a White City, spaciously designed, lighted by electricity, replete with monuments, crowned with public buildings, and dignified by a radiant architecture. The men who planned the exposition knew something about the better side of the spacious perspectives that Haussmann had designed for Napoleon III. Without taking into account the fundamental conditions of industrialism, or the salient facts of economics, they initiated what shortly came to be known as the City Beautiful movement. For a couple of decades Municipal Art societies were rampant. Their program had the defects of the regime it attempted to combat. Its capital effort was to put on a front—to embellish Main Street and make it a more attractive thoroughfare. Here in esthetics, as elsewhere in education, persisted the Brahminical view of culture: the idea that beauty was something that could be acquired by anyone who was willing to put up the cash; that it did not arise naturally out of the good life but was something which could be plastered on impoverished life; in short, that it was a cosmetic.

Until the Pittsburgh Survey of 1908 pricked a pin through superficial attempts at municipal improvement, those who sought to remake the American city overlooked the necessity for rectifying its economic basis. The meanness, the spotty development, and the congestion of the American city were at least in some degree an index of that deep disease of realty speculation which had, as already noted, caused cities like Chicago to forfeit land originally laid aside for public uses. Because facts like these were ignored for the sake of some small, immediate result, the developments that the early reformers were bold enough to outline still lie in the realms of hopeless fantasy—a fine play of the imagination, like Scadder's prospectus of Eden. Here there have been numerous signs of promise during the last decade; but it is doubtful whether they are yet numerous enough or profound enough to alter the general picture.

At best, the improvements that have been effected in the American city have not been central but subsidiary. They have been improvements, as Aristotle would have said, in the material bases of the good life: they have not been improvements in the art of living. The growth of the American city during the past century has meant the extension of paved streets and sewers and gas mains, and progressive heightening of office buildings and tenements. The outlay on pavements, sewers, electric lighting systems, and plumbing has been stupendous; but no matter what the Rotary Clubs and Chambers of Commerce may think of them, these mechanical ingenuities are not the indices of a civilization. There is a curious confusion in America between growth and improvement. We use the phrase "bigger and better" as if the conjunction were inevitable. As a matter of fact, there is little evidence to show that the vast increase of population in every urban area had been accompanied by anything like the necessary increase of schools, universities, theaters, meeting places, parks, and so forth. The fact that in 1920 we had sixty-eight cities with more than 100,000 population, thirty-three with more than 200,000, and twelve with more than 500,000 does not mean that the resources of polity, culture, and art have been correspondingly on the increase. The

growth of the American city has resulted less in the establishment of civilized standards of life than in the extension of
Suburbia.

"Suburbia" is used here in both the accepted and in a
more literal sense. On one hand I refer to the fact that the
growth of the metropolis throws vast numbers of people into
distant dormitories where, by and large, life is carried on
without the discipline of rural occupations and without the
cultural resources that the Central District of the city still
retains in its art exhibitions, theaters, concerts, and the like.
But our metropolises produce Suburbia not merely by reason
of the fact that the people who work in the offices, bureaus,
and factories live as citizens in a distant territory, perhaps
in another state: they likewise foster Suburbia in another
sense. I mean that the quality of life for the great mass of
people who live within the political boundaries of the metropolis itself is inferior to that which a city with an adequate
equipment and a thorough realization of the creative needs
of the community is capable of producing. In this sense, the
"suburb" called Brookline is a genuine city, while the
greater part of the "city of Boston" is a suburb. We have
scarcely begun to make an adequate distribution of libraries,
meeting places, parks, gymnasia, and similar equipment,
without which life in the city tends to be carried on at a low
level of routine—physically as well as mentally. (The bla-
tantly confidential advertisements of constipation remedies on
all the billboards tell a significant story.) At any reasonable
allotment of park space, The Committee on Congestion in
New York pointed out in 1911, a greater number of acres
was needed for parks on the lower East Side than was occupied by the entire population. This case is extreme but
representative.

It is the peculiarity of our metropolitan civilization, then, that in spite of vast resources drawn from the ends of the earth, it has an insufficient civic equipment, and what it does possess it uses only transiently. Those cities that have the beginnings of an adequate equipment, like New York—to choose no more invidious example—offer them chiefly to the traveler. As a traveler's city New York is near perfection. An association of cigar salesmen or an international congress of social scientists, meeting in one of the auditoriums of a big hotel, dining together, mixing in the lounge, and finding recreation in the theaters hard by, discover an environment that is ordered, within its limits, to a nicety. It is this hotel and theater district that we must charitably think of when we are tempted to speak about the triumphs of the American city. Despite manifold defects that arise from want of planning, this is the real civic center of America's Metropolis. What we must overlook in this characterization are the long miles of slum that stretch in front and behind and on each side of this district—neighborhoods where, in spite of the redoubtable efforts of settlement workers, block organizers, and neighborhood associations, there is no permanent institution, other than the public school or the sectarian church, to remind the inhabitants that they have a common life and a common destiny.

Civic life, in fine, the life of intelligent association and common action, a life whose faded pattern still lingers in the old New England town, is not something that we daily enjoy, as we work in an office or a factory. It is rather a temporary state that we occasionally achieve with a great deal of time, bother, and expense. The city is not around us, in our little town, suburb, or neighborhood: it lies beyond us, at the end of a subway ride or a railway journey. We are citizens occasionally: we are suburbanites (*denizens, idiots*) by regular routine. Small wonder that bathtubs and heating systems and similar apparatus play such a large part in our conception of the good life.

5. PROSPECTS OF METROPOLITANISM

Metropolitanism in America represents, from the cultural angle, a reaction against the uncouth and barren countryside that was skinned, rather than cultivated, by the restless, individualistic, self-assertive American pioneer. The perpetual drag to New York, and the endeavor of less favorably situated cities to imitate the virtues and defects of New York, is explicable as nothing other than the desire to participate in some measure in the benefits of city life. Since we have failed up to the present to develop genuine regional cultures, those who do not wish to remain barbarians must become metropolitans. That means they must come to New York, or ape the ways that are fashionable in New York. Here opens the breach that has begun to widen between the metropolis and the countryside in America. The countryman, who cannot enjoy the advantages of the metropolis, who has no center of his own to which he can point with pride, resents the privileges that the metropolitan enjoys. Hence the periodical crusades of our State Legislatures, largely packed with rural representatives, against the vices, corruptions, and follies which the countryman enviously looks upon as the peculiar property of the big city. Perhaps the envy and resentment of the farming population is due to a genuine economic grievance against the big cities—especially against their banks, insurance companies, and speculative middlemen. Should the concentration of power, glory, and privilege in the metropolis continue, it is possible that the city will find itself subject to an economic siege. If our cities cannot justify their existence by their creative achievements, by their demonstration of the efficacy and grace of corporate life, it is doubtful whether they will be able to persuade the country to support them, once the purely conventional arrangements by means of which the city browbeats the countryside are upset. This, however, brings us to the realm of social speculation; and he who would enter it must abandon everything but hope.

Metropolitanism is of two orders. At its partial best it is exhibited in New York, the literal mother city of America. In its worst aspect it shows itself in the sub-metropolises which have been spawning so prolifically since the eighties. If we are to understand the capacities and limitations of the other great cities in America, we must first weigh the significance of New York.

The forces that have made New York dominant are inherent in our financial and industrial system; elsewhere those same forces, working in slightly different ways, created London, Rome, Paris, Berlin, Vienna, Petrograd, and Moscow. What happened in the industrial towns of America was that the increments derived from land, capital, and association went, not to the enrichment of the local community, but to those who had a legal title to the land and the productive machinery. In other words, the gains that were made in Pittsburgh, Springfield, Dayton, and a score of other towns that became important in the industrial era were realized largely in New York, whose position had been established, before the turn of the century, as the locus of trade and finance. (New York passed the 500,000 mark in the 1850 census.) This is why, perhaps, during the seventies and eighties, decades of miserable depression throughout the industrial centers, there were signs of hope and promise in New York: the Museums of Art and Natural History were built: Life and Puck and a batch of newspapers were founded: the Metropolitan Opera House and Carnegie Hall were established: and a dozen other evidences of a vigorous civic life appeared. In a short time New York became the mold of fashion and the glass of form, and through the standardization, specialization, and centralization which accompanies the machine process the Metropolis became at length the center of advertising, the lender of farm mortgages, the distributor of boiler-plate news, the headquarters of the popular magazine, the publishing center, and finally the chief disseminator of plays and motion pictures in America. The educational foundations which the exploiter of the Kodak has established at Rochester were not characteristic of the early part of the industrial period—otherwise New York's eminence might have been briskly challenged before it had become, after its fashion, unchallengeable. The increment from Mr. Carnegie's steel works built a hall of music for New York long before it created the Carnegie Institute in Pittsburgh. In other words, the widespread effort of the American provincial to leave his industrial city for New York comes to something like an attempt to get back from New York what had been previously filched from the industrial city.

The future of our cities depends upon how permanent are the forces which drain money, energy, and brains from the various regions in America into the twelve great cities that now dominate the countryside, and in turn drain the best that is in these sub-metropolises to New York. Today our cities are at a crossing of the ways. Since the 1910 census a new tendency has begun to manifest itself, and the cities that have grown the fastest are those of a population from 25,000 to 100,000. Quantitatively, that is perhaps a good sign. It may indicate the drift to Suburbia is on the wane. One finds it much harder, however, to gauge the qualitative capacities of the new régime; much more difficult to estimate the likelihood of building up, within the next generation or two, genuine regional cultures to take the place of pseudonational culture which now mechanically emanates from New York. So far our provincial culture has been self-fertilized and sterile: our provincial cities have substituted boosting for achievement, fanciful speculation for intelligent planning, and a zaniacal optimism for constructive thought. These habits have made them an easy prey to the metropolis, for at its lowest ebb there has always been a certain amount of organized intelligence and cultivated imagination in New York—if only because it is the chief point of contact between Europe and America. Gopher Prairie has yet to take to heart the fable about the frog that tried to inflate himself to the size of a bull. When Gopher Prairie learns its lessons from Bergen and Augsburg and Montpellier and Grenoble, the question of "metropolitanism versus regionalism" may become as active in America as it is now in Europe.

Those of us who are metropolitans may be tempted to think that the hope for civilization in America is bound up with the continuance of metropolitanism. That is essentially a cockney view of culture and society, however, and our survey of the development of the city in America should have done something to weaken its self-confident complacence. Our metropolitan civilization is not a success. It is a different kind of wilderness from that which we have deflowered—but the feral rather than the humane quality is dominant: it is still a wilderness. The cities of America must learn to remold our mechanical and financial régime, for if metropolitanism continues they are probably destined to fall by its weight.

THE METROPOLITAN MILIEU

Ever since I began walking about the streets of New York, noting its people, its buildings, its industries, its activities, I have planned to write an extensive interpretation of my native city's development. The time to have done this was in 1939, when I returned for a winter's residence, after three years spent mainly in my Dutchess County home; but the mounting menace of fascism drove all such thoughts from my mind. If I never live to write that book, the following essay must serve as a substitute.

The Metropolitan Milieu is a subjective interpretation of the city: subjective in the sense that it is focused in a succession of human personalities, Whitman, Ryder, and above all Alfred Stieglitz; it is an attempt to show how a particular environment not merely molds the human personality but often reactivates it, developing compensatory interests that offset its evils and make possible a fuller human growth.

Much of the material in this essay derives directly from my own experiences and impressions. Through my grandfather, Charles Graessel, with whom I used to stroll about the city up to the age of ten, I had a direct connection with a remoter past, with sweet old Bastian, the German bookbinder on University Place, who loved Leatherstocking, or with the custom bootmaker on Canal Street who still made my grandfather's boots. I saw the sordid seventies through the eyes of my mother, who grew up in a gloomy house that still

and dusty vestibules where, in the seventies, a row of pitchers would be exposed through the night, to be filled with milk in the morning. The crosstown traffic became less important, as the rivers ceased to provide the main entrances to the city; but the tangle of wheels on the avenues thickened: shafts interlocked, hubs scraped, horses reared; presently a bridge was built over Broadway for the pedestrian. The vivacious dangers of congestion had all appeared: exasperated drivers exchanged oaths as deadly as bullets, and gangsters, lining up for fights on the dingier side streets, exchanged bullets as lightly as oaths. Respectable folk hunched their shoulders, lowered their heads, and hypnotized themselves into somnolence by counting sheep: at all events the population was increasing.

Beer saloons, four to as many corners in most parts of the city, brought together in their more squalid forms the ancient forces of hunger and love and politics: "free lunch," "ladies' entrance," and the political boss and his underlings. The main duty of the latter was to protect vice and crime and to levy a constant tax upon virtue in whatever offensive form it might take—as justice, as public spirit, as intelligence. Whisky and beer ruled the wits and the emotional life of the city: whisky for aggressiveness and beer for good-natured befuddlement. Barber shops specialized, until the present century, in painting out black eyes that did not yield to the cold iron of the lamp-post. The swells of course drank their wine convivially at Martin's or Delmonico's; but that was as far from the beer saloon as Newport or Narragansett was from Coney Island. In the nineties Messrs. McKim, Mead, and White began to make over the city for the more polished classes: they designed the Century Club, Gorham's, Tiffany's, and many sumptuous mansions in the city for the new Borgias and Sforzas. But these cultured architects of course remained aloof from the principal buildings of the populace, the tenement and the saloon. The dingy brown front of the saloon, with the swinging doors and the sawdust floors and the slate carrying the day's menu and the soap-decorated mirrors, remained unchanged by fashion for two generations or more, obeying the biological law that the lowest organisms tend to remain stable.

In the seventies, elevated railroads were built; and for miles and miles, on each side of these ill-designed iron ways, which contrasted so unfavorably with those Berlin built only slightly later, tenement houses were planted. Thousands of people lived under the shadow of the elevated, with the smoke of the old-fashioned locomotives puffing into their windows, with the clank and rattle causing them to shout in daily conversation to overcome the roar outside. The oblivi-ousness to low sounds, the indifference to cacophony which makes the ideal radio listener of present-day America, was part of the original acquisition of Manhattan in the Brown Decades. This torment of noise-troubled sleep lowered wak-ing efficiency, depleted vitality; but it was endured as if it were an irremediable fact of nature. In the lull of the ele-vated's thunder, the occasional tinkle of the cowbells of the ragman on a side street, or the solemn I—I—I—I cas' clo's of the second-hand clothing buyer, would have an almost pastoral touch; while Carmen, on an Italian's clanking hand organ, could splash the sky with color.

Within the span of a generation, the open spaces and the natural vistas began to disappear. The older beer gardens, like Niblo's Garden, gardens that had frequently preserved the trees and open space of a whole block, were wiped out: only in the further reaches of the city did they remain, like Unter den Linden on upper Broadway, and like the road-houses which dotted the more or less open country that re-

mained on the West side above 125th Street until the end
of the century. The rocky base of Manhattan, always unkind
to life, steadily lost its filament of soil. The trees in the
streets became more infrequent as the city grew; and their
leaves grew sear before autumn came. Even the great Boulevard above Sixty-fifth Street, which the ignoble Tweed had
planted along Broadway for his own pecuniary benefit, sacrificed its magnificent trees to the first subway; while only
the ailanthus tree, quick growing and lean living, kept the
back yards occasionally green, to gladden the lonely young
men and women from the country, who faced their first year
in the city from hall bedrooms on the top-floor rear of un-
amiable boarding houses. And as the city grew, it grew away
from its old markets: one of the last of these, to prove more
reminiscent of the old than anticipatory of the new, was the
Jefferson Market, with its medieval German tower, at Eighth
Street. Vanishing from the consciousness of most Manhat-
tanites were the open markets that had once brought the
touch of the sea and the country to its streets, connecting
farmstead and city home by means of little boats that plied
the Hudson and Long Island Sound.

The waterfront kept a hold on the city, modifying its character, longer than the countryside did. The oyster stands
remained on South and West streets; and "mast-hemmed
Mannahatta" was still an accurate description up to the end
of the nineties: Alfred Stieglitz has indeed recorded for us
the bowsprit of an old sailing vessel, thrust like a proud
harpoon into the side of our Leviathan. But most of the
things that had made life pleasant and sane in the city, the
old houses, red brick, with their white doorways and delicate
Georgian fanlights, the friendly tree-lined streets, the salty
lick and lap of the sea at the end of every crosstown street,
as Melville described it in the opening pages of Moby Dick

—all these things were disappearing from the eye, from the nose and touch, and so from the mind.

The water and the soil, as the prime environment of life, were becoming "immaterial," that is to say, they were of no use to the canny minds that were promoting the metropolis, unless they could be described in a legal document, appraised quantitatively, and converted ultimately into cash. A farm became for the speculator a place that might be converted into building lots: in that process, indeed, lay the meaning of this feverish growth, this anxious speculation, this reckless transformation of the quick into the dead. People staked out claims on the farther parts of the city in the way that prospectors stake out claims in a gold rush. There was always the chance that some negligible patch of earth might become, in the course of the city's growth, a gold mine. That was magic. In the atmosphere of magic, the desire to get something for nothing, a whole population hoped and breathed and lived. That in reality the environment was becoming unfit for human habitation in the process did not concern the midas-fingered gentlemen who ruled the city, nor did it affect the dull-fingered million who lacked that golden touch: their dreams were framed within the same heaven. Lacking the reality, they fed on the gilded lubricities of Mr. Bennett's, Mr. Pulitzer's, and Mr. Hearst's newspapers.

2. THE CULT OF PAPER

The ledger and the prospectus, the advertisement and the yellow journal, the world of paper, paper profits, paper achievements, paper hopes, and paper lusts, the world of sudden fortunes on paper and equally grimy paper tragedies; in short, the world of Jay Cook and Boss Tweed and James Gordon Bennett, had unfolded itself everywhere, obliterating under its flimsy tissues all the realities of life that were not exploitable, as either profits or news, on paper. Events happened to fill the paper that described them and to provide the daily titillation that relieved a commercialized routine. When they came reluctantly, they were manufactured, like the Spanish-American War, an event to which Newspaper Row contributed rather more than statesmanship did.

Behold this paper city, buried in its newspapers in the morning, intent through the day on its journals and ledgers and briefs and Dear-sir-in-reply-to-yours-of-even-date, picking at its newly invented typewriters and mimeographs and adding machines, manifolding and filing, watching the ticker tape flow from the glib automatons in Broad Street, piling its soiled paper into deep baskets, burying its dead paper in dusty alphabetical cemeteries, binding fat little dockets with red tape, counting the crisp rolls and bank notes, cutting the coupons of the gilt-edged bonds, redeemable twenty years hence, forty years hence, in paper that might be even more dubious than the original loan issue. At night, when the paper day is over, the city buries itself in paper once more: the Wall Street closing prices, the Five Star Sporting Extra, with the ninth inning scores, the Special Extra, All-about-the-big-fight, all about the anarchist assassination in St. Petersburg—or Pittsburgh.

The cult of paper brings with it indifference to sight and sound: print and arithmetic are the Bible and the incense of this religious ritual. Realities of the world not included in this religion become dim and unreal to both the priests and the worshipers: these pious New Yorkers live in a world of Nature and human tradition, as indifferent to the round of the seasons and to the delights of the awakened senses and the deeper stores of social memory as an early Christian ascetic, occupied with his devotions amid the splendid temples of a Greek Acropolis. They collect pictures as they collect securities; their patronage of learning is merely a premature engraving of their own tombstones. It is not the images or the thoughts, but the reports of their munificence in the newspaper, that justifies their gifts. The whole social fabric is built on a foundation of printed paper; it is cemented together by paper; it is crowned with paper. No wonder the anarchists, with more generous modes of life in mind, have invented the ominous phrase: "Incinerate the documents!" That would wreck this world worse than an earthquake.

Beneath this arid ritual, life itself, attenuated but real, starved but still hungry, goes on. Lovers still become radiant and breathless; honest workers shave wood, rivet steel beams, dig in the earth, or set type with sure hands and quiet satisfaction; scholars incubate ideas, and now and again a poet or an artist broods by himself in some half-shaded city square. In rebellion against this arid and ugly new environment, some country-bred person, a William Cullen Bryant or a Frederick Law Olmsted, would attempt to preserve faltering rural delights: a picnic grove here, a park there. Just before the Civil War the building of Central Park began; and despite the raids of political gangsters, despite the brazen indecent robbery of the Tweed gang—so malodorously like the political gangs of our own day—a stretch of green was carved out, not merely carved out, but actually improved, from barren goat pasture and shantydom into a comely park.

Meanwhile, the city as a whole became progressively more foul. In the late seventies the new model tenement design, that for the so-called dumbbell apartment, standardized the habitations of the workers on the lowest possible level, encouraging for twenty years the erection of tenements in which only two rooms in six or seven got direct sunlight or a modicum of air. Even the best residences were grim, dreary, genteelly fusty. If something better was at last achieved for the rich in the 1890's, on Riverside Drive and West End Avenue, it remained in existence scarcely twenty years and was replaced by mass congestion.

During the period we are looking at, the period of Alfred Stieglitz's birth and education and achievement, we are confronted with a city bent on its own annihilation. For New York used its intense energy and its taut, over-quickened life to produce meaner habitations, a more constricted environment, a duller daily routine, in short, smaller joys, than it had produced during the modest provincial period. By denying itself the essentials of a fine human existence, the city was able to concentrate more intently upon its paper figments. It threw open its doors to the Irish of the forties, to the Germans of the fifties and sixties, later to the Italians, and to the Russians and Jews of eastern Europe: the outside world, contemptuous but hopeful, sneering but credulous, sent many of its finest children to New York. Some of them pushed on, to the cornlands, the wheatlands, the woodlands, the vinelands, to the iron mines, the coal mines, the copper mines; while those that remained were forced to huddle in utmost squalor. But the congested East Side, for all its poverty and dirt, was not the poorest part of the city: it still had its open markets with their color, its narrow streets with their sociability and their vivid common life and neighborly help, its synagogues with at least the dried remnants of a common vision.

This New York produced the elevator apartment house at the end of the sixties, and the tall building, called the skyscraper after the topmost sail of its old clipper ships, a little later; and it used these new utilities as a means of defrauding its people of space and light and sun, turning the streets into deep chasms, and obliterating the back yards and gardens that had preserved a humaner environment even when people drank their water, not from the remote Croton River, but from the Tea-water Pump.

The spirit of pecuniary pride was reckless and indiscriminate; it annihilated whatever stood in the path of profit. It ruined the ruling classes as well as their victims. As time went on it became ever more positive in its denial of life; so that in more elegant parts of the East Side today there are splendid "modern" mansions that are practically built back to back, even worse in some respects than the vilest slums on Cherry Street. This negative energy, this suicidal vitality, was the very essence of the new city that raised itself after the Civil War, and came to fullest bloom in the decade after the World War. Beholding it in its final manifestations, a German friend of mine wrote: *Dies ist die Hölle, und der Teufel war der Baumeister.* Men and women, if they survived in this environment, did so at the price of some sort of psychal dismemberment or paralysis. They sought to compensate themselves for their withered members by dwelling on the material satisfactions of this metropolitan life: how fresh fruits and vegetables came from California and Africa, thanks to refrigeration, how bathtubs and sanitary plumbing offset the undiminished dirt and the growing tendency toward constipation, how finally the sun lamps that were bought by the well-to-do overcame the lack of real sunlight in these misplanned domestic quarters. Mechanical apparatus, the refinements of scientific knowledge and of inventive ingenuity, would stay the process of deterioration for a time: when they failed, the jails, the asylums, the hospitals, the clinics, would be multiplied. Were not these thriving institutions, too, signs of progress, tokens of metropolitan intelligence and philanthropy?

But in the end the *expectation* of health and wholeness, like the expectation of honesty and justice, tended within the great metropolis to disappear. In the course of its imperialistic expansion the metropolis, as Patrick Geddes put it, becomes a megalopolis, concentrating upon bigness and abstract magnitude and the numerical fictions of finance; megalopolis becomes parasitopolis, dominated by those secondary pecuniary processes that live on the living; and parasitopolis gives way to patholopolis, the city that ceases effectively to function and so becomes the prey of all manner of diseases, physical, social, moral. Within such a town, graft and corruption are normal processes; the greater part of the population shares the animus of the criminal, applauds him when he "gets away with it," and condones his crime when he is caught red-handed. The city that has good words for its Commodore Vanderbilts and Tweeds and Crokers, to say nothing of contemporary gamblers and shysters who have practiced on an even larger scale, which multiplied these antisocial types a thousand times, is a city in which a deteriorated social life, without elementary probity or public spirit, has become normalized into the accepted routine.

So every profession has its racket; every man his price. The tonsil snatcher and the ambulance chaser and the insurance fixer and the testimonial writer have their counterparts in the higher reaches of the professions. The more universal forms of dishonor become honorable, and graft and shakedowns, like the private toll exacted for automobile and marriage licenses, become so common that they even escape notice. Those who actively oppose these customary injustices and these systematic perversions of law and decency are looked upon as disappointed men who have set their own price too high. Force, fraud, lying, chicane, become commonplaces; the law is enforced by illegal methods, the constitution protected by unconstitutional practices; vast businesses are conducted in "peace" by judicious connivance with armed thugs—now passive blackmailers, now active strikebreakers—whose work proceeds under the amiable eyes of the very agents supposed to combat it. No one believes that the alternative to living with honor is to die with honor: it is easier, it is more comfortable, to live sordidly, accepting dishonor.

In such a city, an honest man looms high. He is a lighthouse on a low and treacherous coast. To attain even a human level becomes, in this megalopolitan environment, an arduous, almost a superhuman, task.

3. EARTH, WATER, SKY, MEN

Any fair picture of New York must confess the underlying sordidness of a large part of its preoccupations and activities. It is not that manufacture and shipping and the exchange of goods are necessarily antivital or antisocial processes: quite the contrary. But when these activities become central to life, when they are themselves perverted to serve chiefly as instruments in an abstract accountancy of profit and power, the human hierarchy of values is displaced; and, as in some perversion of the physiological functions, the head becomes cretinous, and the subordinate members become gigantic *and useless*. What I have elsewhere called a purposeless materialism became the essential principle of the city's life.

One must not flinch, then, from recognizing the dark elements of the picture. But one would have no true image, in fact, no image at all, if one forgot to add the light and colors that define the blackest shape; and even at its worst, these elements were always present. There is, to begin with, the physical magnificence of the scene: the sweep and curve of the bay, the grand spaciousness of the river, the rhythm of the tides that encircle it, the strike of its mica-gleaming schists as they crop out in the park or the temporary excavation, and finally, the proud upthrust of the Palisades themselves. In the very shape of the island is something tight, lean, athletic: a contrast to the glacial till of Long Island, with its fat Dutch landscape, its duckponds, its feathery asparagus beds. The skyscrapers, despite their disorder, have not diminished those positive lines in their stalagmitic upthrust: they are almost as geometric as gypsum crystals. And before the skyscrapers were built, from Brooklyn Heights, from the Palisades, from the Belvedere in Central Park, from Morningside Heights, one could see and feel the hard flanks of Manhattan.

Above all, there is the sky; pervading all these activities is the weather. The sharp crystalline days of early autumn, with intense blue sky and a few curls of cloud, drifting through space like the little jets of steam that were once such characteristic outlets of the older skyscrapers: the splendors of sunset on the waters, over the Palisades, crossing the Brooklyn Ferry, looking toward the Jersey shore from the Brooklyn Bridge; the swift, whiplike changes from heat to cold, from fog to clarity, from the sharp jeweled contours of John Bellini to the soft tones of Whistler and Fuller. Occasionally, too, the sulphurous hell of the dog days, to whip up appetite for the dank clouds in the west and the brave crackle of lightning and the drenching showers. At the other extreme the benignity and quiet of a city quenched by snow: the jingle of sleighbells in the 1890's, the cold flash of electricity on the elevated tracks twenty years later.

The niggling interests of the day might lead to a neglect of these fundamental beauties; but they could not obliterate them. Nature remained, ready to nourish the first person who opened his eyes and breathed in the air—the clear, slightly salt-laden air, gray wings swooping and circling through it. This clear air and this intense sunlight are no small encouragements to the photographer. And the landscape as a whole has definition, a disciplined line: the rocks run as due north and south as the points of the compass, and the very sides of the island, once scraggly, have been shaped by the hands of man into sharp lines, like the margin of a Dutch canal. No matter how great the confusion on the surface, beneath it all, in the rocks themselves is order: no matter how shifty man's top layer, the foundations are solid. If the streets are dingy, there is the dazzle of the sky itself: if the alleys and yards are foul, heavy with ancient dirt, with the effluvia of the sewers or the factories, there is the sanative taste of salt in the first wind that blows from the Atlantic. The cold sea fog in spring, sweeping inland in the midafternoon, calls one to the ocean as imperatively as the proud, deep-throated roar of the steamer, claiming the channel as she passes out to sea. So the ocean and the sky and the rivers hold the city in their grip, even while the people, like busy ants in the cracks and crevices, are unconscious of these more primal presences, save when they read a report in the morning paper, and reach for an umbrella, an overcoat, a fan.

Along with its great landscape, New York has had its men. Even in the worst periods of the city's deterioration, there has always been a saving remnant, that handful of honest souls whose presence might have saved the Biblical cities of the plain.

There was, for one, Walt Whitman himself, "of Mannahatta a son," whose visits to the city, with even occasional public appearances, continued after the Civil War, and whose brief pictures of the city are precious records of its life. Whitman, who had rambled about every part of the city, who knew it coming inward from his native Huntington, from Coney Island when that spot was just a fishing hamlet, from the rocky wilds of the upper part of the island, where he would go walking with Bryant—Whitman knew the city at its best. While he realized the evil significance of so much of its vitality, and the impoverishment of its wealth—see his description of the fashionable parade in Central Park in '79 —he was nourished by it and fed steadily on it, opera, theater, bookstalls, libraries, lecture halls; above all, the million-headed throng on the streets.

Drinking at Pfaff's, loafing on the Fifth Avenue stages with the coach drivers, crossing the Brooklyn Ferry, Whitman had caught something in the common life that was dear and permanent. He who really touches the soil of Manhattan and the pavement of New York touches, whether he knows it or not, Walt Whitman. Beneath the snobbery of the commercial élite there was in New York a genuinely cosmopolitan spirit. In those who like Whitman and Melville were well rooted in the provincial soil, this spirit was capable of reaching out for elements that were still foreign to the new country—the philosophy of Hegel and Schopenhauer, the criticism of Carlyle and Ruskin, the vision of Michelet and Hugo—and transporting them to our unfinished landscape. Melville, who had been a common sailor, and Whitman, a common printer and carpenter, were not caught by the bourgeoisie and debased into accepting their prudent paper routine. Both of them were capable of a passionate aristocracy that reserved for the spirit its primacy in the affairs of men. Whitman's democracy was the prelude to a broader-rooted aristocracy, and none knew that fact better than he.

The Roeblings were in New York, too, during the sixties, and Washington remained on, though an invalid, until the Brooklyn Bridge was finally completed in 1883. Not alone did they compose the poem of granite and steel that is the Brooklyn Bridge, one of the first of those grand native works of art that Whitman had demanded of the sayers and delvers, but they brought that arduous habit of intellectual exertion, that capability for heroic sacrifice on behalf of immaterial things, that strict obligation to self-discipline, which came directly from the great Germany of Kant and Goethe and Hegel, a Germany the elder Roebling—who was a pupil of Hegel's—so well knew. It was right for a New Yorker who was interested in science or engineering to seek Berlin during this period; so that even though Stieglitz was unaware of the fact that he was following in the footsteps of the great engineer who built the bridge, it was as natural for him to go to Berlin as it was for Louis Sullivan, a little earlier, to follow the footsteps of Richardson to the Ecole des Beaux Arts in Paris.

Though none of the new buildings in New York could compare in beauty with the High Bridge, in its original stone form, or with the Brooklyn Bridge, there was a stir in architecture in the eighties and nineties, due chiefly to the work of Richardson, whose influence remained even though he changed his residence from Staten Island to Boston. Beginning with the De Vinne Building on Lafayette Street, an excellent structure created for a scrupulous and craftsmanlike master of printing, the finest works of New York architecture were the series of loft and factory and storage buildings that arose in the eighties: buildings whose round arches, solid stone courses, and subtle brickwork set a mark that few later buildings have surpassed. These buildings, moreover, were better than the very best Europe could show in this department at the same period; and contemporary European travelers of discernment noted and admitted this.

Finally, there was Albert Pinkham Ryder, the most sensitive, the most noble mind that appeared in New York after the war, a worthy companion in the spirit to that other postwar recluse, the author of Moby-Dick. If the bold sunlight of Broadway made its sheet-iron buildings look flimsy and unreal, the moonlight of Ryder's inner landscape gave body to reality: Ryder with his intuitions of human destiny, Death Riding around a Racetrack, with his wistful melodies of love, the vision of Perette, Siegfried and the Rhine Maidens, with his presentation of fate in the little boats with a tiny sheet of sail on a broad moonlit sea, to which he so often returned, this mystic had a strength and a purpose that the ephemeral activities of the outer world did not possess. A benign figure, ranging up and down the streets after dark, penetrating life in its stillness and peace more bravely than those who flung themselves into the noisiest corners of the battlefield, Ryder also became part of the soil of Manhattan. No one can be aware of the rich vitality of the city who does not know its Ryder as well as its Whitman. He needed little from the city; he gave back much.

4. THE LIVING ENVIRONMENT

The problem for the creative mind in the nineties, whether he was a young writer like Stephen Crane or a young man with a passion for photography like Alfred Stieglitz, was to face this New York of boundless misdirected energy and to capture a portion of that wasteful flow for his own purposes, using its force without accepting its habitual channels and its habitual destinations. But there was still another problem:

and that was to conquer, with equal resolution, the gentility, the tepid overrefinement, the academic inertness and lack of passionate faith, masquerading as sound judgment, which were characteristic of the stale, fugitive culture of the bourgeoisie. The genteel standards that prevailed were worse than no standards at all: dead objects, dead techniques, dead forms of worship, cast a morbid shadow on every enterprise of the mind, making mind itself a sham, causing vitality to seem somehow shameful. To put the choice with the crudest possible emphasis, the problem for the creative mind was how to avoid the gangster without turning into the spinster.

Now, during the nineteenth century, great forces were at work in the world. People who prefer the tight securities of the eighteenth century or the adolescent turbulence of the seventeenth century only prove their own timidity and ineptness when they belittle these forces merely because they destroyed old patterns and worked creatively on unfamiliar lines. But if the artist was to become a force in his own right once more, as confident of his mission as the scientist or the engineer, it was important that he should not identify himself with the senseless acts of imperialist conquest, or with the senseless mechanical negation of life. When I use the word senseless I use it in both its usual meanings—first, foolish and stupid, and on the other hand, without benefit of the senses, shut off from the experiences that come through the eye, the hand, the ear, the nose, the touch of the body. For the weakness of the mechanical ideology that had put itself at the service of capitalism—and that colored even the minds that rejected it—was that it had limited the provinces of the senses, and confined its operations to a blind world of matter and motion.

Following partly from this mechanical philosophy, partly from the new routine of industry, the senses were in fact denied and defeated in all the new industrial centers; not least, certainly, in New York, which concentrated the industry and the finance of the Western continent. To become a force in this society, this city, it was necessary to open up once more all the avenues of human experience: to sharpen the eye, quicken the touch, refine the senses of smell and taste, as a preliminary to restoring to wholeness the dwarfed and amputated personalities that had been produced—the Gradgrinds, the M'Choakumchilds, the Bounderbys. In a world where practical success canceled every other aspiration, this meant a redoubled interest in the goods and methods that challenged the canons of pecuniary success—contemplation and idle reverie, high craftsmanship and patient manipulation, a willing acceptance of the emotions and an enlargement of the erotic ritual, a shift from the specialized masculine interests leading to an exploitation of power to the more generalized, more centrally biological interests expressed in love: an emphasis on the ecstasy of being rather than a concentration on the pragmatic strain of "getting there."

In the Bhagavad-Gita, Krishna says that the way to contemplation may be found through action as well as through exercises that are directly meant to intensify and illuminate the spiritual life. And it was by action, by utilizing one of the fine mechanical instruments that had been produced by the scientist and the inventor, that Stieglitz, on returning to New York in the 1890's, approached the world around him and helped restore those values that had been left out of the narrow *Weltbild* of his contemporaries. While Stieglitz, through his very use of the camera, allied himself with the new forces at work in the world, he did not, like those who have denied their own humanity, become smaller through his use of the machine. For mark this: only those who live first and who keep alive have earned the right to use the machine. Those who use machinery because they are incapable of facing the stream of life and directing it, those who seek order in automatons because they lack the discipline and courage to achieve order in themselves, become the victims of their instruments and end by becoming mere attachments to a mechanical contrivance. Not so with Stieglitz: from the beginning the machine was as subordinate to his human direction, through his understanding of its potentialities and capacities, as is the breathing of a Hindu guru. When used thus, as part of man's organic equipment rather than as a substitute for a deficient organ, the machine becomes as integral as the original eyes or legs. Assimilating the machine in this fashion, Stieglitz was armed to reconquer the lost human provinces that had been forfeited by the one-sided triumph of the machine.

In the surviving photographs of Stieglitz's early discovery of New York with the camera, one is conscious at first chiefly of his sure and resolute approach to the outward aspects of the city that had been regarded as "unpaintable," and therefore, in a fashion, as unusable. He watches the changing of the horses on a horse car in a snowstorm; he looks at a row of ugly brownstones or hovers above a maze of railroad tracks in a railroad yard, with the locomotives puffing magnificently at the sky. In his interest in these things, he is on a par with another realist, who used paint as his major medium, rather than photography, Thomas Eakins: but his scope is broader, his interests less traditional. Stieglitz does not, like his Parisian contemporary, Atget, range the city from morning to night, deliberately composing a documentary history of its life, after the fashion of Zola. He not merely observes: he waits; he eliminates; he selects. Certain aspects of the city he touches only by implication. Instead of

merely mining the pitchblende, he extracts the minute parti-
cle of radium, which accounts for the strange behavior of
the entire mass.

There are many parts of New York that Stieglitz ignores
or leaves no record of, parts of it that have not entered his
life or nourished him; there are other parts of his experience, like the grand spectacle of the horse races, which mean
much to him and still are preserved only in a print or two.
It is not for lack of love or interest that the epic of New
York is not caught by his camera, chapter by chapter, as it
unfolds from the nineties onward; to seize this was indeed
part of his conscious intention. But the point is that it is not
the document but the life that made it possible that he
searches for and holds to: and as Emerson says, the essential
fact is unaltered by many or few examples. If one doubts
Stieglitz's awareness of the deeper transformations of feeling and thinking and acting that took place in his metropolis
one need only examine his photographs more carefully. The
external change in the city itself was profound. Within the
darkened alleyways of the financial district, people lost their
sense of day and night; just as they lost the occasional
glimpse of the sky which makes the worst routine bearable.
In the new subways they lost even the sight of the sun over
the roof tops of Manhattan, which had once been theirs from
the ramshackle elevated roads. Nature in its most simple
form, the wonder of the morning and the night, was missing
from the metropolitan routine; and *therefore*—I say "therefore" because such reactions are rarely accidents—these elements establish themselves in Stieglitz's photographs with a
new force.

The chief instrument of photography is light; and the fact
that Stieglitz always worked by natural light, never by artificial light, with its studied arrangements and its temptations

to trickery, is an important one. But all the hours of the day become important to him: so he takes the first night pictures that have esthetic significance. The weather, likewise, is an important element for his vision: hence, too, he takes the first photographs in snow and in rain. He does not have to escape to the country to find nature, any more than he has to escape to antiquity to find beauty, in the way that the purse-proud art collectors of the period, the Mrs. Jack Gardners and the Pierpont Morgans, were doing. All these necessary elements in life were still present in the city, though they had been excluded from the routine of getting and spending. Just as Ryder continued to be in touch with nature when he had his ailanthus tree and his patch of sky, so Stieglitz found the necessary germs of a living environment even in a metropolis that had lost the most rudimentary sense of the soil, and was turning itself, step by step, block by block, into a stony waste.

During the 1900's, too, the city was losing its sense of the rivers, despite the extension of Riverside Park. For sewage pollution had driven the North River shad away and made all other kinds of fish that might be caught noxious; so that the old gaffers with their set-lines and bells had disappeared from the Hudson, along with the groups of happy naked swimmers, and another link with nature was broken, even as later, because of pollution from the oil-burning steamers, the waters of the Lower Bay lost the bluefish and weakfish that had once been so plentiful there. But Stieglitz, not less than Whitman, preserved the sense of the waters surrounding Manhattan. He photographed the ferry boats coming into their slips, the boatload of immigrants, the skyline of Man-hattan from the Jersey shore, with the water establishing a base in the foreground. Water and sky come into his pic-tures, again and again: the river, the ocean, the bathing beach, the rain, the snow, and finally, dominating the whole landscape in every sense, the clouds. Shut out by the tall buildings, shut out by the dark courts of the new apartment houses, the very stars at night put at a distance by the myriad lights of the city, flaring, as Tennyson said, like a dreary dawn—the sky remains under all conditions the essential reminder of nature and the cosmos. In the course of Stieglitz's own development, the sky becomes a more and more essential part of his pictures; and finally, it becomes the symbol whereby Stieglitz unites his sense of the universal order with the sense of the personality, as developed in the relations of men and women.

In the stoniest pavement of the city there are cracks. And out of the bleakest soil, between these cracks, a few blades of grass will sooner or later show, whose seeds are borne by the birds; here, even, the germ of a tree will take root and spring up, if no foot disturbs it. It is in the cracks between the new buildings that Stieglitz finds the sky; it is in the surviving cracks in the pavement that Stieglitz finds his trees; and in his most characteristic pictures of the city, so far from emphasizing the massiveness and the obduracy of its stones, he emphasizes the presence of life. One of the most moving and impressive pictures he ever made was that of a little tree in Madison Square Park, young and vernal in the rain, with a street sweeper in the foreground and the dim shape of a building in the background: the promise of life, its perpetual reawakening and renewal, are in that print.

Wherever Stieglitz turns his head in this city, he looks for the touch of life, seizes it, emphasizes it; and by this means he sets himself in opposition to those who would glorify the negation of life and sanction its subordination to metropolitan business, material concentration. Meanwhile, all the forces of urban aggrandizement are on the make: advertising, insurance, and high finance, the divine trinity that rules the world of industry and perverts its honest labors for its own ends, gather together in the city and out of its egotism and self-inflation rose higher and higher skyscrapers, first in the southern end of the island, then, forming a sort of double vertebral column, from Thirty-fourth Street upward, in the new central district. The new office buildings and lofts are flanked by apartment houses as stupidly planned, as extravagantly designed, as crazily and as dishonestly financed as the business buildings themselves. The megalopolitan architects who designed these puerile structures gloated over the prospect of a whole city composed of skyscrapers, with aerial drives for the rich, and in the murky canyons below the working and living quarters for the poor—artificially lighted! artificially ventilated!—a city in which sunlight would be supplied by sunlamps, grass by green tiles, and babies, presumably, by mechanical incubation. (No extravagance of Aldous Huxley's satire was beyond the serious commonplace luncheon conversation of the self-infatuated schoolboys who were financing and planning and building the "city of the future," on paper.)

A generation after his first pictures of New York, Stieglitz surveys the city once more, now from the seventeenth story of an office building at Fifty-third Street, surrounded by the architectural bluff and fraud of the boom period. He ironically portrays these structures with no further hint of nature than the indication of the hour of the day, through the degree of light and shadow that falls on their trivial facades. He shows the skyscraper—the mock city of the future—in the last state of mechanical perfection and human insignificance, devoid at last of even the possibility of earning money: financial liabilities, as well as the social liabilities their reckless misuse had already made them. There, in effect, is the ultimate result of putting nature at a distance and subordinating all the values of living to the paper routine of pseudo-work and profit-pyramiding. These skyscrapers of Stieglitz's last photographs might be the cold exhalations of a depopulated world.

And at the end, with a sardonic gleam in his eyes, he photographs the turning point: the tearing down of a seven-story building at Sixtieth Street and Madison Avenue in order to make way for a new two-story building. The nightmare was over. The human scale had begun to return. Finally, the sterile dream of imperialist conquest externalized itself in that last gesture of the impotent: Rockefeller Center. But this was already an aftermath, which, like an auto rolling backward downhill, continued on its course because the driver preferred the sensation of motion, even if it were motion backwards, to the recognition of his inability to reverse the direction and go forward.

5. SYMBOLS OF VITALITY

While the tree and the sky are dominating symbols in Stieglitz's work, brought to sharper focus by their steady exclusion from the urban landscape, there are two others that were important, both in his personal life and in his vision: the race horse and the woman. The thoroughbred horse, quivering in every muscle, nostril open, eyes glaring, hooves delicately stamping, ready for the race or the rut: symbol of sheer animal vitality, bred and nurtured with a single eye to that final outburst of speed which carries horse and rider down the home stretch to victory. From the black heavy-flanked Waterboy or the low-slung, short-legged chestnut Sysonby, to the great Man o' War and his present-day successors, these horses represented the pinnacle of animal achievement: proofs of man's skill and intelligence in alliance with the world of life, symbolic of those new strains of wheat, those new hybrids or sports in flowers and fruits, whose conquest was ultimately more important to man than were half the mechanical contrivances on which the metropolitan mind doted.

And if the horse was animal vitality, woman was—if one may combine the words—animal spirituality, that form of spirit which, unlike the lonely ascetic endeavors of man, fulfills itself in the very organs of the body, in the warmth of the arms, in the tenderness that emanates from the breast, in the receptivity of the lap, in the utilization of every physical fiber for the higher ends of life, making the body not the enemy of the mind but the friendly guide and initiator; favoring the warm intellect, touched by the earth, the intellect of Goethe, as contrasted with the cold intellect, the intellect divorced from the earth, the intellect of womanless men like Leonardo. Man tends to overvalue his eyes and his muscles: the organs of definition and of physical conquest. Woman teaches him to use his lips, his sense of touch, and to diffuse some of the fierce tactile sensitiveness that is at first concentrated so exclusively in his generative organ. Here is a vitality even deeper-fibered than that of the thoroughbred horse; for it reaches, through the very structure of woman's body, toward a completer biological fulfillment, never being fully organized or alive except when the relationships lead, through the lover or the baby, to the ultimate breast and womb.

The masculine world, with its strife of markets, with its stultifying ambitions to corner wheat or to cheapen steel, to invent this or that substitute for organic life, to conquer by an equation or a formula this or that territory of the intellect, this masculine world, particularly in our own cultural epoch, has tended toward an asceticism that has left little energy or time for the fundamental biological occupations. The seed was sound and fruitful: the great outburst of vitality marked by the rising birth rate of the nineteenth century proved it: but the soil was too dry and sour and lacking in humus to give the plant itself full growth. So that it was the classes at the periphery of our mechanical civilization, more often the not-serious people, the unbusinesslike, the wastrels and gamblers and sports, the "low" and the "vicious," among the males, who still preserved an alert eye appreciative of the flanks and fetlocks and neck of a horse, or the flanks and belly and buttocks of a woman.

Compare the stock exchange and the race track. Economically, both are mainly gambling devices; and humanly speaking they are both low forms of activity. But one is indoors; it is conducted in a clamorous jumble of noises by means of a series of telegraphic symbols; the realities with which the gamble deals, the automobile factories and packing plants and mail-order houses and banana plantations, are present only as verbal abstractions. The other activity is held outdoors under the sky; the track, heavy or fast, is affected by accidents of the weather; the gamble has to do with visible horseflesh and visible human skill and courage; and in the procession to the post, the suspense of the start, the stretching out of the field, and the final climax of the home stretch, there is a superb esthetic spectacle. The drama itself does not terminate abruptly with the end of the race: the tension is prolonged by the return of the jockey to the judge's stand, where he awaits for an instant, with upraised arm and whip, the nod that gives him the victory in a fairly won race.

Dégas came closer than anyone else among the painters to representing this drama; but there is something, in the four-dimensional continuity of it, that evades even the most skilled of painters; indeed, the impulse to grasp this continuity was responsible for the critical steps in the invention of the motion-picture camera. At the bottom of this interest is the horse himself; and until the automobile usurped this interest, the horse and the gambling connected with the races were ways in which the American, caught in his artful commercial merry-go-round, kept a little of his residual sense of the primitive and the organic. Right down to the end of the first decade of the present century, the Speedway at 155th Street was maintained as a common race track for trotters; and the designer of Central Park, a generation earlier, was forced, in the interests of more general recreation, to plan his horse drives so as to curb racing.

If Stieglitz did not photographically utilize this deep interest of his in the horse races—there is, however, the fine print of Going to the Post—it was only perhaps because its intensity was incompatible with that patient suspended animation which makes photography possible. Stieglitz was too near the race horse, as one is too near the lover in an embrace, to be able to photograph him. And yet the horse symbolized to him, as it did to the author of St. Mawr and to the author of Roan Stallion in a later generation, something essential in the life of man: that deep animal vitality he had too lightly turned his back on and renounced in his new mechanical preoccupations. So Stieglitz conceived, though he never carried out, a series of photographs of the heads of stallions and mares, of bulls and cows, in the act of mating, hoping to catch in the brute an essential quality that would symbolize the probably unattainable photograph of a passionate human mating.

6. SEX AND LOVE

Just as the old rural interest in animals could enter the city only deviously by way of the race track, so sex itself, despite its endless manifestations, had no central part in the routine of the civilization that had reached a mechanical apex in New York. Where sex was most obvious, in the burlesque houses and musical comedies and in the murky redlight district, it was also most furtive and shamefaced: a grudging admission, not a passionate conviction; an itch, not an intensity; a raw piece of flesh flung to a caged animal, who responded in his reflexes, like a Pavlovian dog, without benefit of mind. Foreign observers noted that women tended to dominate the pioneer society of America, and to hold its males in nominal subservience to ideals of courtesy and chivalry toward womanhood. But although the traditional scarcity of women in a new country gave woman a privileged position and permitted her a freedom of travel and a freedom of choice in mating unknown among similar classes in Europe, the result was to widen the political scope of woman at the expense of her sex life. Instead of ruling with and through her sex, the American woman, despite her studious attention to her own beauty, her figure and her dress, learned to preserve her freedom and power by keeping sex at a distance. It was on the assumption that "nothing could happen" that the sexes came together so easily, and that women in America, up to the second decade of the present century, were given their "freedom."

And in any fundamental sense nothing did happen, even after the American girl extended her flirtations to the length of concluding them in bed. The whole business of sex remained peripheral: sexual expression symbolized freedom or sophistication; indeed, it often sank so low as to justify itself as hygiene. People married and became the parents of children and were driven to seek divorce before they had even scraped the surface of intimacy. This negation of sex was helped, perhaps, rather than hindered by the devices of birth control. Contraceptive devices put between passion and its fulfillment a series of mechanical or chemical obstacles which, though small in themselves, could never be completely routinized into oblivion: the least objectionable device from the standpoint of intercourse was also the most dangerous in the possibilities of serious lesion. If this is still largely true today, a hundred years after the initial movement toward birth control in America, it was even more true a generation ago, when the crudeness and uncertainty of the various devices used added to the clumsiness and anxiety that attended their employment. With sex, the dish often became lukewarm before it could be served; and with the loss of warmth and flavor went a loss of appetite; for why, if the final result were favored by lukewarmness, should people ever bother to reach in the first place a hotter temperature?

Lusty men and passionate women of course remained in this society; but the whole tone of sex remained practically as low as it had been in Victorian days. Although talk about sex, and even possibly physical indulgence, became more common, the actual manifestations often remained placidly anemic: a girl might have a dozen lovers without having known an orgasm, or have a dozen orgasms without having achieved any fundamental intimacy with her lover. On the surface, decorum or the defiance of decorum; beneath it, irritation, frustration, resentment—resentment on the part of the male for the unarousableness of the female, about whom the faint aroma of anxious antisepsis clung like an invisible petticoat; resentment on the part of the female against the male both for his bothersome insistence and his lack of really persuasive aggression. In the course of business, the work in the office and the factory, the activities of the home, the club, the social gathering, men and women saw each other too little on their more primitive levels to overcome all these obstacles and find each other. They sought by the chemical means of drink to reach these levels more quickly—only to lose the sting and sharpness of sex, when what they needed was patience and leisure and sympathy and above all free energy and vitality, for all of which a tumescent animal befuddlement was in no sense a substitute. For what was left for sex but the dreary crowded moments before sleep, when all energy had been spent upon every aspect of living except sex?

One emphasizes the state of sex in American society because here again Stieglitz was to preoccupy himself with symbolic representations of the elements that were lacking in the scene around him. As a young student in Europe, he had found his own sense of manliness and sexual confidence reinforced and cultivated by the great traditions of the arts, above all by Rubens, whose portrait of Hélène de Fourment, an exuberant naked girl wrapped in fur, he had seen on his first visit to Vienna, at a critical moment when it had re-echoed and eloquently justified the impulses he found within himself. The health, the animal vitality, the unashamed lushness of sex in Rubens's paintings, are all as conspicuous as the absence of these qualities in the unhealthy sentimentality that has hung around sex in the Western world, since Christianity attempted to transfer to heterosexual relations the sick moonlight glamour of unfulfilled yearning that derived ultimately, perhaps, from the romantic homosexual love of the Greeks. Rubens was a long step back to reality from the misty mid-regions inhabited by Poe's pallid maidens, girls who were reproduced in paint in the adolescent sweetness of George Fuller's paintings in the seventies, and still further attenuated in the popular Dewing ladies who ruled the nineties. The ideal maiden of adolescent America was a sort of inverted pariah: untouchable by reason of her elevation. In defiance of Nature, her womanliness and her untouchability were supposed to be one. But what was sex, how could it exist, how could it nourish the personality, if it were not in fact the most essential demonstration of touchability—if the intercourse of lovers, at all its levels, from the intuitions at a distance to the final stages of union, were not accompanied at every moment by that direct sense of touch, that tact, which removes the need for words and signs and breaks down the formidable distance between object and subject, between thine and mine?

In all the meanings of the adjective, sex was primarily the realm of tactile values. Stieglitz was to discover these values and intensify them in his photography even before Berenson had used them, too narrowly, as a key to the great painting of the Italian Renaissance. The blindness of love, debased as a mere figure of speech, is indeed one of the most characteristic of its attributes. It is blind in the fact that it reaches deeper levels of consciousness, below the open-eyed rationality of practical achievement. It is blind in the way that it often shuts out the outer world in order to concentrate upon the inner stimulus, blind as in terror, blind as in prayer; and finally, it has the beautiful compensation of blindness, for it learns to see with its fingertips, and to offset the closed eyes, reacts more quickly with the other available senses in every region of the body.

It was Stieglitz's endeavor, at first mainly instinctive, finally, through a better self-knowledge, with a fuller awareness of his actions, to translate the unseen world of tactile values as they develop between lovers not merely in the sexual act but in the entire relationship of two personalities —to translate this world of blind touch into sight, so that those who felt could more clearly see what they felt, and so those who could merely see might reach, through the eye, the level of feeling. Observe the work of Stieglitz's contemporaries in photography, moved perhaps by the same desires but deeply inhibited. See, in the many reproductions in Camera Work—which doubtless helped pave the way to the sun-bathing and easier nudity of a later day—see how they portray the nude body. However honest their efforts, they nevertheless surround the body with a halo of arcadian romanticism; note how resolutely they equip their naked models with glass bubbles; how they compel these naked girls painfully, for the first time in their lives, to pour water out of narrow-necked jugs; how they lash them to tree stumps or make them shiver at the edge of icy pools. Sex must be disguised as art—that is, as artiness—before one may peep at it without blushing. Undisguised, the girl averts her face from the camera, so that the self-conscious and self-righteous face shall not acknowledge the powers of the body. The efforts of these earlier photographers are not to be despised; but the tantalizing fear of sex, a fear of its heady realities, is written over their pictures, with their dutiful aversions, their prescribed degrees of dimness, their overarch poses.

It was his manly sense of the realities of sex, developing out of his own renewed ecstasy in love, that resulted in some of Stieglitz's best photographs. In a part-by-part revelation of a woman's body, in the isolated presentation of a hand, a breast, a neck, a thigh, a leg, Stieglitz achieved the exact visual equivalent of the report of the hand or the face as it travels over the body of the beloved. Incidentally, this is one of the few aspects of photography that had not been antici- pated in one fashion or another by the painter, since the dismembered anatomical studies of the Renaissance, which casually resemble these photographs, are purely instruments of factual knowledge: they make no appeal to sentiments and feelings. In more abstract, yet not in less intimate form, Stieglitz sought to symbolize the complete range of expression between man and woman in his cloud pictures, relying upon delicacies and depths of tone, and upon subtle formal relationships, to represent his own experiences. Earth and sky, root and topmost branch, animal intimacy and spiritual expression—these things, which were so remote from the routine of the metropolitan world, or which there existed in such loud disharmony, were restored to their natural integrity in Stieglitz's life and work. What was central became central again; what was deep was respected for its profundity, instead of being ignored; what was superficial was thrust behind the essential.

Stieglitz was never a better son of the city he loved and identified himself with than when he turned his back on her desiccated triumphs and recalled, in word, in photography, in the tenacious act of existence, the precious elements that the city had excluded. With Whitman, with Ryder, with the handful of other men that each generation has produced in New York, Stieglitz has served his city, not by acquiescing in its decay, nor yet by furthering its creeping paralysis: he has served it by nurturing in himself, and in those who have witnessed his work, the living germs that may reanimate it, quickening the growth of the higher forms of life it has excluded. Here, indeed, life goes on and renews itself.

MASS-PRODUCTION AND HOUSING

*While this essay does not deal directly with the planning
of cities, it makes an analysis of what is, from the standpoint
of quantity and social importance, the most important factor
in city growth: the building of homes. As early as 1902 Mr.
H. G. Wells, with his great flair for technological analysis,
had outlined the prefabricated house of the future in his
Anticipations. But at the time my essay was written (1929)
discussion of the prefabricated house was still a novelty.
With an obstinacy worthy of a better cause, those who
fancied that prefabrication offered an easy way out from all
the thorny problems of co-operative planning and distribu-
tive justice, made promises and prophecies that the next
fifteen years were to prove spurious.*

*My attack on these fantasies of salvation by a blind imi-
tation of the automobile continued throughout the thirties;
but I cannot pretend that the points I made in the two articles
I have here printed as one—which originally appeared in the
Architectural Record—were understood, much less heeded,
by the enthusiastic and often fanatical minds that regarded
prefabrication as a cure-all. Even intelligent business men
seem to have lost any sobering contact with cost accountancy
when they approached this problem.*

*In the main, my analysis merely follows the masterly
demonstrations of the late Henry Wright, with whom I had
the honor to be closely associated from 1924 onward: with*

Albert Mayer, we were co-founders of the Housing Study Guild in 1933. What Henry Wright had discovered about housing costs in general I applied to the problem of prefabrication. As the reader will note, I deny neither the possibility nor the value of prefabrication: what I deny is the notion that it will by itself solve the problem of housing. Recent experience has only underlined the convictions I expressed fifteen years ago. On the Vallejo Project in California, the experimental site-fabricated houses designed by William Wurster proved cheaper in the cost per unit than the factory-fabricated houses, though the latter were in quantity production.

My plea for an organic many-sided attack on the problem of housing is one that I would stress again today, in view of the tendency of public authorities as well as builders and manufacturers to tie themselves down to a set of wooden formulae, more concerned with paring down first costs than with establishing reasonable costs over the whole period of the house's existence: more concerned with narrowing the needs of the occupant than with meeting them on broader and more humane terms. But if I were to rewrite this article with a view to present conditions, I would place an even greater emphasis on the need for regional diversity in our plans for housing, and the wastefulness, accordingly, of planning the distribution of prefabricated houses on a national scale, from models worked out in terms of the greatest common demoninator.

As for those old-fashioned minds that still think that a house should be a movable object, so that man, instead of being a free-living animal, should creep about the world like a snail, with a house on his back, there is no reasoning with them: the covered wagon in one age and the trailer in ours both have their specific uses; but neither is an answer to man's need for a stable domestic habitation and a communal environment. One does not solve the problems of living in a civic community by encouraging wholesale nomadism. Where the advocates of the self-contained house have gone astray is in their disparagement of the need for the community; they show contempt for the co-operations and solidarities made possible only by living together with one's neighbors and making use of man's collective facilities, his libraries, hospitals, churches, schools and political associations. Much of what has passed for hard rationalistic thinking among the advocates of a purely mechanical solution is nothing but irresponsible romanticism, indeed, anarchic individualism: a use of the machine to deny the collectivity that has made the machine possible. That sort of thinking is as fatal an indication of the flight from reality as the political isolationism of a Charles Beard or the evasive "pacifism" of a Frank Lloyd Wright.

[This paper first appeared as two articles in The Architectural Record, Jan.-Feb. 1930; and it is reprinted with the Record's kind permission.]

---

1. THE BEGINNINGS OF FABRICATION

During the last hundred and fifty years a great change has taken place in architecture. This change has nothing to do with the questions of superficial esthetics that agitated the architectural world: the quarrels between the classicists and the medievalists or between the traditionalists and the modernists are all meaningless in terms of it. I refer to the process whereby manufacture has step by step taken the place of the art of building, and all the minor processes of construction have shifted from the job itself to the factory.

How far this process has gone everyone is aware who has watched the composition of a building, and who knows how suddenly the whole work would stop if the architect were forced to design or specify with any completeness the hundred different parts, materials, and fixtures he draws from Sweet's Catalog. But what are the implications of this process? What results must it have on the status of the architect and the place of architecture in civilization? What further developments may we look forward to on the present paths: what alternatives suggest themselves?

Some of these questions can be answered: others will lead us to push beyond the current premises upon which the discussion of mass-production and architecture is based.

By an ironic accident, the first use of fabricated parts in a building seems to have been ornamental: the plaster moldings of the eighteenth century were introduced before the Franklin stove: but the age of invention ushered in a whole series of technical devices designed to increase the comfort or the efficiency of the dwelling house, and along with these improvements went a shift from handicraft to machine production. There are country districts in the United States where, until a few years ago, the kitchen sink would have been made of sheet zinc fitted over a box made by the carpenter, or where the icebox might have been constructed in the same way. In the main, however, the shift was steady and inexorable: steam heating, gaslighting, electricity, baths, toilets, refrigerators, to say nothing of radio-connections and garages, have all led to the industrialization of architecture. Plaster, jig-saw, and cast-iron ornament, the first spontaneous gifts of industrialism, all happily diminished; but the technical improvements remained and multiplied.

In the great run of modern building, except in part the country homes of the rich, mass-manufacture has taken the place of local handicraft. The latter has remained in two places: the construction of the physical shell itself, and the assemblage of the individual parts.

Now, this change was coincident with the withdrawal of the architect from the grand body of building during the early industrial period. The new factories and bridges and railroad stations were largely the work of engineers, while the great mass of private dwellings became the province of the speculative jerry-builder who, with a few stereotyped plans, created the dingy purlieus of all our large cities. The radical change that had taken place passed almost unnoticed, until during the last fifteen or twenty years the architect was called in to design small houses for industrial villages. He was then confronted with two brute facts: if he designed houses for industrial workers in the fashion that he did for the upper middle classes, it turned out that the costs were so high that only the middle classes could afford to live in them: that was the fate, for example, of Forest Hills, Long Island. On the other hand, when he accepted the price limitations laid down by the industrial corporation, or, as in Europe, the municipal housing scheme, he suddenly discovered that he was no longer a free man. Every variation he wished to introduce which departed from current practice was prohibitive in cost: his design was in fact little more than a composition of standardized patterns and manufactured articles. The elements were no longer under the architect's control; for the carpenter on the job could not construct a kitchen cabinet as well or as cheaply as the factory, nor had he spent so much time in finding out exactly what compartments and divisions the housewife preferred. As for windows, doors, bathroom equipment, the architect either had to accept them as they came from the factory, or he had to do without them altogether.

2. MECHANICAL ABSORPTION OF ECONOMIES

Needless to say, this revolutionary change had come about without any genuine renovation in design, and without any attempt to overcome the difficulties that the increase of manufactured articles brought with it. The chief of these difficulties, as Mr. Henry Wright was perhaps the first to point out, was that the building proper, without being cheaper in its own right, accounted for only 45 to 60 per cent of the total cost, whereas a hundred years before it had represented, with its decoration and ornament, about 90 per cent of the total cost. Some accommodation to this condition was made; but the adjustment was a blind and fumbling one: now it came as jerry-building, a general cheapening of materials and workmanship, again it came as smaller rooms or fewer rooms per family, or finally, it came as an abandonment of handicraft on the remaining parts of the building, and the increase of ready-made equipment. Decoration had not so much vanished by itself, for lack of artistic talent, still less because of any doctrinaire prejudice against it: it had rather been absorbed by, or at all events transformed into mechanical fixtures. The new costs of finance, mechanical fixtures, utilities, had to be met at some point in the design. Short of a proportional rise in the real income of wage-earners, there was no way of cementing the old requirements and the new in a single building.

In a word, building has shrunk, manufacture has expanded. One cannot suppose that this process will stop short at the shell. Apart from the fact that this has already been partly conquered—as yet, however, with no appreciable saving—in the mail-order wooden house, or in the sheet-iron garage, who doubts that the manufacturers of steel, aluminum, or asbestos blocks, if not the large-scale motor manufacturers, looking for a new outlet for a market glutted with cars, will finally produce a light transportable shell, whose sections will be set up easily by unskilled labor? It would not be difficult to describe such a house: indeed, Mr. Buckminster Fuller in Chicago and the Brothers Rasch in Germany have already gone a step beyond this. The chief difference between the factory-manufactured house and the current product of the jerry-builder in Flatbush or West Philadelphia would be that in the first case the design would possibly bear some living relation to the elements out of which it is composed. The mass-house would probably be placed on a platform, if not on a pedestal, in order to provide garage space and avoid the expensive cellar; the plans would be standardized; the pipes and fittings and fixtures would be integral with the walls and ceilings, joined together by a turn of the wrench; and the use of light insulating materials would both facilitate transportation and permit the design of large windows which would otherwise, in cold weather, make a great drain on the heating system.

What would be the advantages of the completely manufactured house? There are many potential ones. First of all, the mass-house, like the motor car, will be able to call to its design and construction a corps of experts, sanitary engineers, heating engineers, hygienists, to say nothing of professors of domestic science, who will have their minds focused, not upon solving indifferently an indeterminate number of problems, but upon getting a perfect solution for a fixed and limited problem. These research workers will have the opportunity to deal with fundamental mechanical and biological facts, without the distraction of attempting to compose these facts into a traditional frame, conceived when industry and family life were on an entirely different basis, and when the inventions of the last century were still but vague grandiose dreams in the minds of Utopians like Leonardo and Johann Andreae.

The introduction of this council of experts would undoubtedly hasten the rationalization of the modern house. A dozen standard plans, with all minor deviations ruled out, would probably take the place of the competitive chaos that provides our more traditional forms of monotony and squalor, or, as in the well-to-do suburb, of standardized "variety" and fake elegance. No one would be able to pretend that individuality and personality are achieved by meaningless departures on the drafting board from standard dimensions: once the mechanical requirements were granted, an equally mechanical solution would follow. The charm of good building, the charm due to the carpenter's or the mason's feeling for his material and site, would disappear; but as compensation there would be the austere clarity of good machinery; and since this charm is already a sentimental memory in most of our building, it is an illusion rather than a reality that would be destroyed. Undoubtedly the result would be "hard"; but such hardness is surely preferable to the spurious "softness" of imitation half-timbers, imitation slates, and imitation fires; and it would constitute a real improvement over the actual quarters in which a great part of the population now lives.

There is no need to go here into the various technical improvements that may be possible in the mass-house. It is enough to assume that such matters as artificial cooling and heating, the removal of dust, and the utilization of sunlight would receive competent attention, and it is even possible that entirely untried methods, such as the heating of walls by electric grids, or complete insulation from outside air would be tested, if not incorporated in the mass-house. Such dwellings would represent a real advance from the standpoint of hygiene and constructive soundness; and since a good part of our population needs to be re-housed, its present quarters being unsanitary, crowded, vile, ugly, and entirely out of key with the best features in the modern environment, the mass-house holds out, on the surface, very attractive promises. Does the architect shrink from the prospect? He had better not. As a profession he has permitted something far worse than the scientifically designed mass-house, namely the unscientific one of the jerry-builder, to appear; and since he has shown as yet no capacity to face or master the real problem of housing, he cannot in all conscience turn away from this spectacle.

3. HOW GOOD AND HOW CHEAP?

Let us grant, then, the mechanical advantages of the mass-house; and along with this its practicability. We must now ask another question: to what extent would the mass-production of such houses be a solution of the housing problem, and how far would this form of manufacture meet all the needs that are involved in the dwelling house and its communal setting? Those who talk about the benefits of mass-production have been a little misled, I think, by the spectacular success of this method in creating cheap motor cars; and I believe they have not sufficiently taken into account some of its correlative defects. Let us consider a few of these.

First of all: the great attraction of the manufactured house is the promise not only of efficiency but of cheapness, due to the competitive production of houses in large quantities. It is doubtful if this will prove to be a great element in reducing the cost of housing. The reason is simple. The shell of the building is not the largest element in the cost;

the cost of money, the rent of land, the cost of utilities, including streets, mains, sewers and sewage disposal plants, are among the major items on the bill. The two new spots where mass-production would take the place of present methods, namely, in the shell itself, and in the assemblage of the parts, offer only a minor field for reductions. To cut the cost of the shell in half is to lower the cost of the house a bare 10 per cent. The New York State Housing and Regional Planning Commission has shown that the lowering of the interest rate 1 per cent would effect as great a reduction; and the lowering of it to the level justified by the safety and durability of housing investments would reduce the costs far more drastically than the most ingenious cheese-paring on the structure.

Moreover, with respect to the other parts of the house, the fixtures, the mechanical apparatus, the finish, it remains true that while slight economies are possible through further standardization, a good part of these items is already produced by mass-methods—and most of the possible economies have been wrung out. Novelties in plan or design, such as those suggested in the Dymaxion house, should not obscure the fact that the great change in the shell is only a little change in the building as a whole. For lack of proper cost accounting our experimental architects have been butting their heads against this solid wall for years; but there is no reason why they should continue. Land, manufactured utilities, site-improvements, and finance call for a greater share of the cost than the "building" and labor. Mass-production will not remedy this. To use cesspools instead of sewers, artesian wells instead of a communal water system, and cheap farming land instead of urban land, as some of the advocates of the manufactured house have suggested, is merely to camouflage the problem: and it is more than a little naïve: for such expedients are temporary dodges, which may occasionally be favored by a sandy soil or inaccessibility to traffic, but they cannot count for two pins in any comprehensive and universal solution of the housing problem. There are many districts where an artesian well would cost as much as the house itself; and except in a communist society there are no spots on the earth where the Law of Rent is not operative—so that any large movement towards the open land, such as is now taking place fifty miles from New York, is immediately recorded in a conversion of farmland into building lots, with a swift rise in price. In short: the manufactured house cannot escape its proper site costs and its communal responsibilities.

The second hole in the program is the fact that mass-production brings with it the necessity for a continuous turnover. When mass-production is applied to objects that wear out rapidly, like shoes or rubber tires, the method may be socially valuable, although the late Thorstein Veblen has shown that some of these potential economies are nullified by the commercial habit of weakening the materials in order to hasten the pace of destruction. When, however, mass-methods are applied to relatively durable goods like furniture or houses, there is great danger that once the original market is supplied, replacements will not have to be made with sufficient frequency to keep the original plant running. Our manufacturers of furniture and motors are driven desperately to invent new fashions in order to hasten the moment of obsolescence; beyond a certain point, technical improvements take second place and stylistic flourishes enter. It will be hard enough, in the depraved state of middle-class taste, to keep our mass-houses from being styled in some archaic fashion, pseudo-Spanish or pseudo-Colonial, as the fad of the day may be; and once mechanical improvements bring diminishing returns this danger will be a grave one.

There is still another defect in the manufactured house, just the opposite of the tendency to foist new style, in order to increase the turnover. One might call this the model T dilemma. Mass-production, just because it involves the utmost specialization in labor-saving machinery and the careful interlinkage of chain processes, suffers, as I have pointed out elsewhere, from rigidity, from premature standardization. When the cheapening of the cost is the main object, mass-production tends to prolong the life of designs which should be refurbished. In the case of the dwelling house, the continuance of obsolete models would possibly be as serious as surface alterations of style; and it is hard to see how mass-production can avoid either one or the other horn of this dilemma. At best the mass-house promises a better mechanical integration. That would constitute an advance; but not an overwhelming one; and the mere ability to purchase such houses easily and plant them anywhere would only add to the communal chaos that now threatens every semi-urban community.

4. THE PRESENT DILEMMA

What, then, is the conclusion? So far as the manufactured house would base its claim upon its social value, that is, upon the possibility of lowering the cost of housing to the point where new and efficient dwellings could be afforded by the owners of Ford cars, its promises are highly dubious. Granting every possible efficiency in design or manufacture, the mass-house, without any site attachments, would still represent an expenditure of from six to ten times the amount invested in automobiles of similar grade; and this leaves us pretty much in our present dilemma. The new houses might well be better than the present ones—they could scarcely be worse. But, if better, they would not be radically cheaper, and since a new cost, a cost that is excessive in the motor industry, namely competitive salesmanship, would be introduced, the final results promise nothing for the solution of our real housing problem—the housing of the lower half of our income groups, and particularly, of our unskilled workers. The manufactured house no more faces this problem than the semi-manufactured house that we know today.

This does not mean that the processes of manufacture will not continue to invade the modern house; nor does it mean that the architect's present position in relation to the problem is a happy one. The question is whether he is able to devise an approach to the housing problem and to house design which will bring with it all the efficiencies promised by the Brothers Rasch or by Mr. Buckminster Fuller, and which will at the same time give scope to the particular art and technique of which he is master. Is there perhaps a more radical approach to the problem of housing than the engineer and the mechanical-minded architect have yet conceived? I think there is; for though Mr. Fuller, for example, believes that he has swept aside all traditional tags in dealing with the house, and has faced its design with inexorable rigor, he has kept, with charming unconsciousness, the most traditional and sentimental tag of all, namely, the free-standing individual house. If we are thorough enough in our thinking to throw that prejudice aside, too, we may, I suspect, still find a place for the architect in modern civilization.

We have now to see whether there is not a different line of advance which rests upon a more thorough comprehension of all the social and economic as well as the technical elements involved. Without abandoning a single tangible gain in technique, there is, I think, a more promising road that, so far from eliminating the architect, will restore him to a position of importance.

Taking the individual house as a starting point, it is by now hopeless to attempt to restore it to a central position in domestic architecture. The individuality of such houses is already lost. Except for a bare 10 or 15 per cent of the population, such houses cannot be produced by individual architects, attempting to meet the unique wishes of a special client. The words Colonial, Cotswold, Tudor in suburban architecture are mere attempts to cover by literary allusion the essential standardization that has taken place; and as soon as we approach the price level of the ordinary run of house dwellers, clerks, salesmen, skilled industrial workers, to say nothing of the more unskilled operations and the more poorly paid trades, the game is already lost; the manufactured shingle, the roughly turned colonial ornament, or the plaster "half-timber" show the strain on the purse.

Admirable as is the layout, the pervading conception, of our first American attempt at a "town for the Motor Age," for example, no candid critic can pretend that the individual one-family houses in Radburn are particularly triumphant examples of modern architecture; and the reason is that even with large-scale organization and limited dividends, it is impossible to isolate such houses sufficiently and lavish upon them the attention that so graciously humanized the traditional house even as late as 1890. Architecturally, these studiously suburban types fall down badly beside the finer rows and quadrangles of Sunnyside, the work of the same architects; and if anyone thinks he can do better with the cheap free-standing house, let him try it.

The isolated domestic unit cannot be made sound, beautiful, and efficient except at a prohibitive cost. If we wish to retain the single-family house, we shall have to accept it as a completely manufactured article; and in this event, we must throw overboard every sentimental demand. The advocates of the single-family house have never faced this dilemma: they dream of universalizing the work of Mr. Frank Forster or Mr. Julius Gregory; but the sort of domicile that their ideas actually effectuate for the majority of the population are the dreary rows of West Philadelphia and Astoria.

5. THE ECONOMIC ALTERNATIVES

Now, a careful economic analysis shows that there are four possibilities from among which we must choose, if we are to have the renovated domestic architecture we so badly need, namely:

We may reduce the cost of housing from 30 to 40 per cent by foregoing all the mechanical utilities we have introduced during the last hundred years. This would enable us to spend enough upon the structure and the materials to produce a fairly good-looking traditional house. As a practical feat, this could be accomplished only in the country; and nobody would regard it as a serious remedy for the urban housing problem: so we may dismiss it.

Or, second: we may raise the wages of the entire industrial population to such an extent that they will be able to make a demand for houses of the same grade that the upper middle classes now create. This is not entirely outside the bounds of possibility; but it would necessitate an economic revolution, not alone in the distribution of incomes, but in a maintenance of the entire industrial plant up to the pitch of wartime productivity. Since we cannot create decent single houses for the relatively comfortable middle class today, it is doubtful if this could be accomplished even under an energetic and efficient communism. In order to make good housing practicable, the wages of the lower income groups will indeed have to be raised, either directly or under the disguise of a subsidy; but no rise will bring back the one-family house in an urban area that possesses a complete municipal and civic equipment, including waterworks and sewers and schools.

Or, third: we can preserve the individual isolated unit at the price of accepting all the limitations that now accompany it: lack of open spaces, scantiness of materials, lack of privacy, rapid deterioration of equipment, and lack of esthetic interest. Some of these evils would be mitigated or removed completely in the ideal manufactured house; but other evils—as I showed earlier—would remain under our current system of commercial production.

Or, finally, we may seek to establish an integral architecture. This means that instead of beginning with one aspect of the architectural problem, we will begin with the community first, and treat the problems of economics, community planning, technics, and architecture as one, seeking a solution not in terms of the individual "cell" but in terms of the larger unit. This last scheme would derive the character of the house or apartment from the particular social whole of which it is a part; and the solution would not be a fixed quantity, but a variable, adapted to soil, climate, landscape, industrial conditions, racial groupings, and the whole remaining complex that makes up a human community. Instead of crabbing our solution by asking before anything else how shall the single-family house be preserved, we ask the broader question: how shall the fundamental requisites of domestic life be embodied in a modern community program—and that is a radically different matter.

The last course is the only one that really sweeps the board clear of preconceptions and inherited prejudices and faces the problem of the house as it comes before us in the Western

world in the year 1930. Unfortunately, there is a considerable vested interest opposed to it: not merely the interest of
the small builder, used to doing things in a small way, or
the individual home-buyer who has been vainly dreaming of
the twenty-thousand-dollar house he will some day buy for
half that price with a thousand dollars down and the balance
in installments, but against it are such organized bodies as
the "own-your-own-home" movement, to say nothing of a
good many sincere and honest people who have concerned
themselves with the evils of congested housing. We have all
these groups, to say nothing of the standard Fourth-of-July
orator, to thank for the notion that the free-standing individual house must be preserved at any cost, as if "home"
and America were inconceivable without it.

Most of the arguments that support this sentiment are spe-
cious and fundamentally unsound; but they still carry an air
of respectability. The individual free-standing house was as
much a product of the Romantic movement as Byronic col-
lars: it was the formal counterpart of the completely free
and isolated "individual," and to look upon it as an im-
memorial expression of the "home" is to betray a pretty
complete ignorance of human history—an ignorance that one
can condone only because an adequate history of the dwelling house in all its transformations has still to be written.*
Spurred on by this romantic conception of the home, its
partisans blindly cling to the poor mangled remnant of a
free-standing house that remains in the outskirts of our great
cities, rather than face the fact that these dwellings are sardonic betrayals of all the virtues they profess to admire, and

---

* Since 1930, Mr. A. F. Bemis' study, The Evolving House, has appeared; but Vol. I, A History of the Home, deals almost exclusively with
the detached, isolated unit and neglects the collective units—rows and
tenements—which have played such a large part in both European and
American history.

possess scarcely a single tangible advantage. Under the cloak
of individuality, personality, free expression, the partisans
of the free-standing house have accepted the utmost refinements of monotony and unintelligent standardization.

Unfortunately, intelligent planning and design on a community scale cannot proceed until this prejudice is knocked
into a cocked hat. It is not until the architect has the courage
to reject the detached house as an abstract ideal that he will
have the opportunity to embody in his designs some of the
advantages and beauties that are supposed to go with such
a house. That is the paradox of modern architecture: we can
achieve individuality only on a communal scale; and when
we attempt to achieve individuality in isolated units, the
result is a hideous monotony, uneconomic in practice and
depressing in effect. We have sometimes succeeded in our
synthetic buildings, the hospital, the office building, the apartment house and the domestic quadrangle: we fail, we shall
continue to fail, in the isolated house. In the first part I
pointed out the economic and mechanical reasons for this
failure; and I have now to suggest in concrete terms a more
favorable program of work.

6. TOWARD INTEGRAL PLANNING AND DESIGN

The aim of an integral architecture, like the aim of the
purely mechanical and constructivist architects, is to effect
an economy which will raise and spread the standards of
the modern house. Where is this economy to be effected,
and how is it to be embodied in design? It is here that the
difference in approach between the two methods comes out.
Are we to attempt to incorporate in the individual house all
the improvements made possible by a communal technology,
duplicating every item as we now duplicate radio sets and
vacuum cleaners, or shall the individual cell be simplified

and the costs of all our new mechanical devices distributed through the whole group of cells, careful community planning being used to reduce the cost of equipment?

A concrete example will perhaps make the difference in approach a little clearer. Take a matter like the supply of fresh air. Apart from any human pleasure that may come from the gesture of throwing wide the window and taking in a breath of purer or cooler air, there is no doubt that the problem of pure air can be mechanically solved by means of an artificial ventilating system, which will clean, humidify, and warm at the same time. In certain places and under certain circumstances this system is highly desirable; but, however practicable it is, no one can doubt that its extension to the dwelling house would only add one further element of expense to that vexatious column of expenses which has been lengthening so rapidly during the last thirty years. Instead of working in this direction, an integral architecture, for the sake of economy, would endeavor to secure through site planning and site development, through orientation to sunlight and wind, a result that can otherwise be obtained only through an expensive mechanical contrivance. In a word: the mechanical system accepts all the factors in house production as fixed, except the mechanical ones: an integral architecture looks upon all the elements as variables and demands a measure of control over all of them.

This demand may seem to pass beyond the limits of pure architecture, and the architect may be reluctant to make it. No matter: he will be driven to it for the reason that the house itself has passed beyond the limits of mere building. The modern house functions as a house only in relation to a whole host of communal services and activities. The rate of interest, the wage-scale, the availability of water and electricity, the topography and the character of the soil, and the community plan itself, all have as great a control over the design as the type of building material or the method of construction. It is fantastic to think that adequate design is possible if all these other elements are determined by forces outside the governance of either the architect or the community. There are, accordingly, two critical places which the architect must capture and make his own if he is to solve the social and esthetic problem of the modern house: one of them is the manufacturing plant, and the other is the community itself. With the part that the architect has still to play in industrial design, I cannot deal here; but something must be said further of the relation of modern architecture to the work of the community planner.

The unit, bear in mind, is no longer the individual house, but a whole neighborhood or community; and the place where collective economies are sought is not merely in factory production, but at every point in the layout or development. In Europe, where a serious attempt has been made, particularly during the last ten years, to cope with the housing of the industrial worker, such schemes are usually fostered by an existing municipality, as in Amsterdam and London, since there are no constitutional limitations upon the housing activities of cities in most European states: in America, apart from dubiously paternal attempts at better housing, undertaken by mill towns, the integration of architecture and community planning has been the work of the limited dividend corporation, such as the Russell Sage Foundation or the new City Housing Company, or the more farsighted real estate developers, such as the founders of Roland Park in Baltimore.

The right political and economic form for modern community building is perhaps one of the most important social questions that architecture must face; all the more because there is no likelihood that private capital will enter the field whilst fabulous profits can be wrung out of less vital business enterprises. The instigation of such enterprises is not the private job of the architect; but it is a public matter where the weight of professional opinion may legitimately be thrown on the side of the public interest. Plainly, the architect cannot solve by any magical incantations the problem of supplying new houses to families whose income is not sufficient to cover the annual charges. There is no answer to that question except, as I said earlier, in the form of higher wages or state subsidy; although a willful blindness to this fact is almost enough to establish a person as a housing authority in the United States. An integral type of architecture, seeking economies at every point in the process, is possible only when the necessary corporate housing organization has been erected.

Economy begins with the selection of the site itself, since the modern city, with its underground articulation, cannot be cheaply produced on a rocky or extremely irregular terrain. The next step is in the design of the street and road system. Here the differentiation of domestic neighborhoods from commercial or factory areas, and their permanent protection through easements, restrictions, and zoning of the land, not alone keeps the land-values low—since there is no speculative temptation through possible changes of use— but reduces the cost of paving and utilities connections. Mr. Raymond Unwin made a great advance in community planning over twenty years ago, when he proved that there is "Nothing Gained by Overcrowding" since the burden of multiple streets beyond a definite point more than counterbalances the apparent economy of more numerous lots; and Mr. Henry Wright has more than once demonstrated that there is enough wasted street space in the average American neighborhood to provide it with an adequate park—a demonstration which has now been effectively embodied in the plan of Radburn. The grouping of houses in rows and quadrangles, instead of their studied isolation, is a further factor in economy, not merely by making the party wall take the place of two exterior ones, but by reducing the length of all street utilities, including the paving of the street itself; and the result is a much bolder and more effective architectural unit than the individual house.

With control over these exterior developments, the problem of the interior economies is reduced and simplified; indeed, the two elements are co-ordinate in design, and if architects produced their work on the site instead of in the office, and did not habitually conceal the site costs from their clients—as "additional charges"—they would long ago have perceived this. Emerson said that one should save on the low levels and spend on the high ones; and one cannot improve upon this advice, either in living or in the design of houses. It is a mistake in esthetic theory to assume that the demands of vision and economy, of esthetic pleasure and bodily comfort, always coincide; and an important task of integral architecture is to balance one against the other. Where the means are limited, the architect must exercise a human choice between, say, an extra toilet and a balcony, between a tiled bathroom and a more attractive entrance.

This choice cannot be made on any summary abstract principle; it is determined by a multitude of local individual factors: the presence of mosquitoes or the absence of large open spaces may, for example, decide the fate of the balcony. If the architect be limited in such local choices, he may have to spend riotously on mechanical equipment; if he have a free hand in community planning, he may let nature take the place of an extra heating unit, an awning, or what not.

Again: if a family is forced to look out upon a blank wall, as so many rich people must do on Park Avenue or Fifth, expensive moldings, draperies, fineries may be necessary to relieve the depression of the outlook: if, on the other hand, sunlight and garden-vistas are available, a wide window may take the place of much footling architectural "charm."

In sum, mass-production which utilizes all the resources of community planning is capable of far greater and more numerous economies than mass-production which only extends a little farther our current factory technique. Such a program for the modern house holds out no spurious promises of a quick, ready-made solution for the difficulties that have been heaping up in every industrial community for the last hundred and fifty years. On the contrary, it isolates the problems of housing which are immediately soluble, from those that can be solved only through a drastic reorientation of our economic institutions; and it paves the way for necessary changes and adaptations in these institutions. If we are to modernize the dwelling house and create adequate quarters for our badly housed population—a far more important remedy for industrial depression than merely building roads —the architect must bring together all the specialized approaches to this problem, instead of merely trying to catch up with the latest specialty. The correct attack was initiated during the war in the governmental war housing program; it has been carried further during the last ten years, by architects and community planners such as Messrs. Stein, Wright, Ackerman, Kilham, Greeley, and Nolen; and although the designs of these men have so far kept close to traditional forms, their approach gives promise of a vital architecture which will in time surpass the work of the present pioneers as their own work surpasses that of the jerry-builder.

REPORT ON HONOLULU

The test of an idea consists in its ability to meet the issues of real life and provide a rational basis for practice and action. In that sense, the following Report on Honolulu is a proper appendix to The Culture of Cities. The invitation to make the report, indeed, came as a result of the interest that book awakened in the Chairman of the City and County Park Board, Mr. Lester McCoy, and his brilliant architectural collaborator, Mr. Harry Sims Bent. Without the help, understanding, and experience of these two friends, this report would not have been conceived nor could it have been written.

When I went to Honolulu in June, 1938, I had only two purposes in mind: to relax from the pressure of writing and to give two addresses to a conference of the International Fellowship for Education, at the invitation of the able secretary of the Progressive Education Association, Mr. Frederick Redefer. About Hawaii itself I had been skeptical; from the distance it seemed only a romantic movie set. But the first nine days I spent there proved to be the most intense, the most esthetically vivid, the most intellectually rewarding I have perhaps ever spent anywhere: so it required very little to persuade me to return with my family in August for a more intensive survey of its native resources and its urban possibilities.

The Hawaiians, who have sweetened and gentled all the

races that have flowed together in the Islands, even the hard-bitten missionaries, even the puppet-wired Japanese, still retain, mid the sordor of the new civilization, much of the charm that Melville had found in their fellow-Polynesians in the Marquesas. Some of their life-wisdom I tried to incorporate in this report; and I hope it deserves in some slight degree the compliment that my first radio talk on Honolulu evoked in an old Hawaiian woman who remarked to a friend of mine: He loves Hawaii like a Hawaiian and he speaks like a true one.

The late Lester McCoy was a beautiful specimen of an almost vanished breed: a public-spirited Tory who lived by his principles. On some of the most fundamental matters of religion and politics we were completely at odds; but men of principle have something important in common even when their principles differ: each knows on which side of the line he is fighting and each knows the extent of their common ground. A little before settling down to the final drafting of this report I sought to find out from Mr. McCoy the sort of topics he thought should be covered, to be sure he accepted my own interpretation of my duties. His answer should be engraved in every administrator's heart: "When I ask a professional man for advice," he said quietly, "I don't want him to tell me what is in my mind: I want to find out what is in his." Needless to say, the man who spoke these words printed the report without challenging a word in it; and he loyally circulated it and backed it up. Eventually he resigned his chairmanship when my own drastic proposals for the reorganization of the Park Board found no favor among his colleagues.

The other fruit of this midsummer journey was a shorter report on the development of the Pacific Northwest, written at the invitation of Mr. B. H. Kizer of Spokane, a great citizen and a great regional statesman. I had planned to fol-low that up with a closer and more comprehensive survey in 1940; but the disasters that confronted the world then made me turn aside from planning to write Faith for Living. And so, to my regret, I have nothing comparable to show on the development of that other fascinating environment: the Pacific Northwest, and in particular, the Columbia River Basin. Some day I still hope, if only as a souvenir of the friendship and love I bear Ben Kizer, to make an extensive report on the possibilities of regional culture in the diverse lands of the Douglas fir and the bull pine, from rainy Port-land to the dry desert air of Spokane.

---

1. HONOLULU'S UNRIVALED SITUATION

All good planning must begin with a survey of actual resources: the landscape, the people, the workaday activities in a community. Good planning does not begin with an abstract and arbitrary scheme that it seeks to impose on the community: it begins with a knowledge of existing conditions and opportunities. It seeks to bring out and to develop further latent advantages; and it seeks to import from other areas useful goods that happen to be lacking in the natural scene, as Hawaii has for long been adding to its great store of trees and plants: but above all it seeks to conserve re-sources that are already in existence and to bring them to a higher pitch of perfection. In the course of this development, art—as the conscious expression of human design—has a decisive role to play: wherever man settles, he displaces raw nature with something that bears the marks of his own mind and his own interests. But art has been defined as the well doing of that which needs doing; and so it is important to recognize "what needs doing," as a first step toward doing it better. Much that is weak in our current practices is a result, not of anti-social action or of perverse intentions, but of sheer indifference and ignorance.

Honolulu is the natural stage for a complex and beautiful human drama. The blue sea, the jagged mountains, the rhythmic roll of the surf over the coral reefs, and the tumbling clouds form a landscape that has few rivals as a setting for human activity. But the city itself has taken its splendid physical features in a somewhat casual fashion. Honolulu is a little like a beautiful woman, so well assured of her natural gifts that she is not always careful of her toilet: she relies upon her splendid face and body to distract attention from her disheveled hair, her dirty finger nails, or her torn skirt. Up to a point, such careless self-confidence is admirable; but Honolulu is now like a beauty passing into middle age, who can no longer be quite sure of drawing people's eyes to her unless she is smart and well-groomed and radiantly in health. The wrinkles are beginning to show; the old wardrobe has ceased to be just quaintly old-fashioned; much of it is now in disreputable tatters. Worst of all, Honolulu has now reached a point where some of her natural advantages are not merely in danger of being neglected: they have already been spoilt. More disastrous results may follow unless steps are taken at once to conserve Honolulu's peculiar advantages.

What are the main conditions imposed by the earth, which must underlie all of man's plans and contrivances here? The first great gift is the wide stretch of beach and shallow water, which is broken to form the natural channel and entry to the port. The sea permeated the life of the original Hawaiians:

their love of bathing, their mastery of swimming, their delight in surf-riding, their studious perfection in fishing, have
remained as a lasting link between their ancient ways and
the less primitive life lived by the various haole * groups
that have followed. The display and daring exercise of the
body, in all the sports connected with the water, is one of
the permanent attractions of Honolulu. And one may safely
assert that any development of the city that ignores or threatens to impair these attractions works against its best interests.

Another great natural resource of Honolulu, which gives
it a value for permanent residence that far surpasses many
other tropical or semi-tropical regions, is its equable climate.
This is due to the trade winds that sweep over the city from
the northeast: this forms the most admirable air-cooling
apparatus that a community could boast. Whereas in tem-
perate climates the elemental principle of good planning is
to command the fullest possible exposure to sunlight, in a
climate like Honolulu's, with its open-air life, the main
effort must be to temper the torrid sun and to achieve the
utmost degree of ventilation. This does not merely mean
open houses: it means an open and oriented type of planning,
of which Honolulu as yet can show but few good examples.

Not the least of Honolulu's interesting natural conditions
is its characteristic downpours of rain, and the corresponding
need of an extensive system of surface drainage to take care
of the run-off of water, not alone in the rainy winter months,
but even at odd moments at other seasons of the year. A large
part of the low-lying areas of the city was originally swamps
and duck ponds. The belated building of adequate drainage
canals shows how slowly the need for coping seriously with
this condition was recognized. As yet, the challenge that this

* White; foreign.

problem offers has been taken up and carried through in only one great planning project: the Ala Wai Canal. The precedent set in that development is so good that it may well set a pattern for other similar situations: it is an excellent illustration of the way in which a utilitarian need, like that for drainage or for highway circulation, may, through imaginative design, be converted into a permanent delight.

The fourth great natural feature of Honolulu is its vegetation. Viewed from the top of Punchbowl, for example, the city is one of the most parklike of cities: the density and spread of the foliage give a deceptive appearance of spaciousness, even where in fact the trees overarch a huddle of filthy shacks. This parklike quality of Honolulu owes much to the typical brilliance of its tropic foliage, the pepper red of the poinciana, the brilliant yellow of the golden shower, the feathery greens of the palms, the dark tones of the banyan trees. One might define Honolulu as a great park, partly disfigured by a careless weedy undergrowth of buildings: indeed, vegetation takes the place of fog in other climates in hiding the city's architectural misdemeanors. One of the chief problems in re-planning the city as a whole will be to make this appearance of universal verdure as effective in fact as it seems to the eye.

In every city, a perpetual contest goes on between the garden and the desert. The streets of the city tend—through overcrowding, through congestion of traffic, through indifference to all but the barest physical needs—to become a stony waste: an environment hostile to life: noisy, dusty, ugly, unsafe. In such an environment, bare health can be maintained only by heroic exertion. The garden, on the other hand, as the aristocracies of the world have always known, is a life-favoring environment: gardens renew the air, temper the heat of the sun, reduce the glare and strain, provide visual delight, give space for play and relaxation and one of the most sanative of all modes of work—the care of plants itself. It is not by accident that the healthiest type of city that has been designed in modern times—one of the few whose health rates and mortality rates equal those of the neighboring countryside—is the Garden City. To make park and garden a permanent attribute of the modern city is one of the chief contributions for the modern planner.*

One further natural resource needs to be canvassed: the people of Honolulu themselves, and the various cultures that meet and mingle here in their daily practices. The original Polynesian culture has left a beneficent trace on the entire life: its kindly human sense, its love of healthful natural activities, its nutritive diet must all be reckoned with in any intelligent planning scheme. The high Oriental cultures that have also left their mark on the city, through the Japanese and the Chinese, have a no less powerful contribution to make: already they have begun to influence the architecture; and their ceremonious cult of beauty, especially in their cultivation of flowers, has reinforced the original Hawaiian inheritance. Finally, the systematic rationalism of the Western world, with its habits of close accountancy of time, money, and energy, has contributed an element of purposive activity that perhaps helps to counterbalance the more indolent, haphazard ways that are closer to the life-rhythm of the tropics. Hawaii is a significant experiment in that hybridization of cultures which will perhaps mark the future development of human society: it is a miniature experimental station. Not the least of the resources that must be conserved through

---

* By "Garden City" here I mean specifically Letchworth Garden City and Welwyn Garden City in England, laid down in accordance with the principles enunciated by Ebenezer Howard in Garden Cities of Tomorrow: a classic work. Only in ignorance may the term be applied to a suburban development or to the principle of open planning.

good planning is the population itself. For the ultimate work of art in any community is the man and the woman that the landscape and the culture produce.

Here, then, is a situation that holds many unusual advantages for city development. What use has been made of them?

2. HONOLULU'S PLANNING ASSETS

When one points out the defects in the development of a city, its citizens sometimes exhibit resentment: they have adjusted themselves to these defects, they are often unconscious of them, and at times they even incline to class them with benefits. The inertia of habit, the indifference of repetition, underly the citizen's apparent sense of pride. People sometimes look more benignly on familiar evils than they are inclined to look upon unfamiliar goods.

Such complacency is unsound and debilitating; and one may remark that this resistance to improvement does not usually characterize the same person's attitude toward a new motor car. The cure for it is perhaps to point out the elements over which the citizen may legitimately congratulate himself. In Honolulu, such a list of good things would begin with the fact that the city, though overgrown, has not gotten completely out of hand: its 150,000-odd inhabitants afford all the variety of group and personality necessary for a flourishing city. It is a city that has not altogether forfeited its contact with earth, air, sky: even though the beach fronts have been stripped to almost nothing, people still maintain the right to fish and swim there; even though the houses are crowded, it is hard to find a district so mean, a shack so wretched as to lack the sight of some growing plant. It is a city of low houses: even its business district has escaped the

blight of the skyscraper, though Waikiki is marred by two
gawky hotel structures. In the residential streets the narrow
service road is common: the super-block and the cul-de-sac
are not unknown. These are economical devices of modern
planning, which one must approve in principle, even while
one may question the particular manner in which they have
been planned. Even the concentrated holding of land would
have advantages, if the owners of such land were as socially
and architecturally enlightened as the great ground landlords who built up Bloomsbury, Mayfair, and Belgravia in
London between the seventeenth and the nineteenth centuries.
The very fact that so much of Honolulu is built of wood, and
that so many of its old structures need to be renewed, should
further the process of change: whereas in cities that have
sunk too much of their capital in steel and stone, the resistance to change becomes as massive as the buildings themselves.

In short, Honolulu is a city that has only to learn how to
conserve and utilize its natural advantages to remain one of
the most attractive spots on earth: it is a city where, if the
social and esthetic vision needful for planning ever took
possession of its leaders, a transformation might be wrought
that would lift Honolulu beyond all rivalry. No other city
that I know would proportionately yield such high returns
to rational planning as Honolulu. But the necessary impulse,
the necessary popular support, will be lacking so long as
Honolulu's citizens seek to maintain the system of familiar
compromises, evasions, and negligences that are recorded in
the present state of Honolulu. In the end, who loves his city
best: he who seeks to improve it or he who is content to
muddle along in the familiar grooves, exercising a minimum
of foresight, intelligence, and imagination? History allows
no doubt as to the answer: that which makes a city dear to

later generations is the power to master its own destiny and express its best ideals in the transformation of its environment.

3. MAJOR WEAKNESSES IN HONOLULU'S PLAN

Though the indigenous life of Honolulu is close to the water, the city plan scarcely discloses that fact. The cluttered development of shipping and marketing facilities around the docks indicates that no attempt has been made to clear away and order the space needed for approach to the docks, and for the expeditious unloading of goods. Except for the very recent development of Ala Moana Park and for very brief stretches elsewhere, it is impossible to skirt the waterfront either on foot or by car. No attempt has been made, curiously, to preserve the approaches to the water to give vistas of the sea at the end of the makai-pointed * streets and avenues: too often the old streets swerve and cut off the vista. Bishop Street is potentially one of the fine business streets of the world; and the major element that contributes to its beauty is that its lower end shows the harbor in a frame of palm trees. Many of the streets that parallel Bishop Street lack this connection; and even Bishop Street is too narrow, and too scantily planted, therefore, to achieve the maximum effect. Even in farther parts of the city, not least in Waikiki, this sense of the waterfront is lacking. The visual neglect of the water has been a conspicuous defect in the development of Honolulu's Street Plan. Hence the need for a waterfront parkway: hence the need of occasional broad boulevards leading down to the water.

The failure to make use of the trade winds on both the city plan and the conventional site layouts is equally inept.

* Makai means seaward in Hawaiian; mauka, mountainward. These terms are in universal use in Honolulu.

One of the great principles of modern town planning is that of orientation: choosing the direction of the streets and the building sites so that sunlight and breezes can be used to greatest advantage. Because of the place that the trade winds have in making life comfortable here, orientation should be strictly observed in site layouts: blocks and houses should be so set that currents of air will flow freely through them. From a glance at the street plan of Honolulu, it is plain that this principle never entered for a moment into the calculations of the real-estate subdivider or the municipal engineer. Not merely are the streets and houses arranged higgledy-piggledy, but the houses themselves, chiefly because of high land values and exorbitant rents, are placed too closely together: as if to prevent adequate circulation of air. Open building, with a coverage of the lot area at which 40 per cent would represent the topmost coverage allowable, is characteristic of modern planning. Such open building is desirable in every part of the world; but it is nothing less than a vital necessity in Honolulu. Without it, adequate gardens are impossible and the private lanai, even when provided, is stuffy. So far from taking this natural condition as a determinant of plan, the greater part of Honolulu's buildings, not excepting some in its more expensive residential areas, overcrowd the land on which they stand. This throws an extra burden upon the parks system, which must not merely perform its normal duties, but make up in part for the deficiencies in open spaces in the private areas of the city.

The relation between open planning, air circulation, and efficiency is worth extra emphasis here. In a well-organized factory, like that of the Hawaiian Pineapple Company, the principal working units are designed so as to permit the free circulation of the air. Numerous physiological investigations, beginning with Winslow's classic experiments, have shown that the lowering of the temperature is not so important as the direct air cooling of the body. Mechanical air conditioning may be a useful auxiliary to nature under special conditions; but for the mass of the population, and for most circumstances of living, the natural modes of air conditioning that would be available to everyone in the city through adequate planning must retain major importance.

The third great weakness in Honolulu's development is the spotty and erratic nature of its growth. Large tracts of land near the middle of the city have long been held out of use: this has prevented the orderly and systematic development of the city, section by section, and it has necessitated a premature building up and exploitation of the land in the remoter suburban areas. This has been accompanied by the extremely costly development of the hillside sites of the city, long before, in the ordinary course of things, they should have been made available. In tracts like that of St. Louis Heights, for example, land has been opened up to middle-class home owners who could ill afford the excessive street paving and utility costs that such a development calls for: and the city has been forced to expand its municipal services at a disproportionate cost. In many cases, the original owners lost their entire savings in the process of liquidation that followed.

Most private citizens are completely unaware of the relation between site costs and the total cost of building a house. They are unaware that irregular parcels of ground are more expensive to grade and service than even parcels; that the amount spent on putting sewers and water mains in hillside areas is disproportionately high; and they are even more innocent of the fact that the over-extension of streets and utility mains, in contrast to a more compact and consecutive development from the center outwards, is one of the major causes of municipal deficits—indeed, bankruptcy. When funds are lacking to provide safe traffic intersections, necessary street lightings, or new schools, they do not connect this shortage with money that has been unwisely spent elsewhere, on servicing subdivisions that cannot in reality pay their way. Unfortunately, many city officials, financiers, and real-estate subdividers are equally ignorant—and equally indifferent as to the economic and social results of a reckless policy of expansion.

Not merely has the original land-holding system placed an obstacle in the way of Honolulu's rational development. In addition to this, no systematic attempt has apparently been made, during the last thirty years, to correct the haphazard methods by which the land has been platted and connected together, or to anticipate the growing needs of intercommunication between the various parts of the city. The congestion of the traffic in the central area is a common phenomenon in most American cities: it points to the need for a radically different type of street design, in which the street will no longer be called upon to serve as a parking area, and in which by-pass avenues will take part of the traffic load away from those streets which locally serve the business section. The lack of a clear connection between the Ewa and Waikiki sides of the town is aggravated by the hideous bottleneck of congestion that now exists on the makai side.

While ample arterial parkways are lacking on the makai and mauka sides of the city, no serious attempt can be made to solve Honolulu's traffic difficulties; and as far as the park system goes, this means that on the days of heaviest park use, access to the recreation areas is obstructed to wheeled traffic, and the value of the recreation period itself is partly undermined by the extra time and nervous energy spent in going to and from the parks. Despite this fact, which should be evident to every citizen of Honolulu, considerable support has been obtained for the highly dubious Pali Tunnel project, whose cost, whose upkeep, and whose tendency to further disorganize the growth of the city should put it far down on the priority list of public improvements—or remove it altogether. Meantime, the planning of internal parkways for the city, which would radically improve the circulation through the area and make accessible all its facilities, is scarcely even discussed.

Let me note one last weakness in Honolulu's development. Partly because of natural conditions, partly through an historical development, the city divides itself naturally into a series of major zones: the port zone, the industrial zone, the central shopping zone, the administrative zone, the recreation zone, and the residential zones. The amount of area available for these various types of zone seems more than adequate to present needs; and it will probably be equal to future demands. What is badly needed, however, is a further clarification of these natural zones. An attempt should be made deliberately to push industry away from the waterfront on the Waikiki side of the port, in order to keep a uniform approach to Waikiki and to give the proposed Civic Center site a more harmonious background. Lack of vigilance here has already permitted a spotty and ill-kempt development, in which the excellence of some of the new individual pieces of architecture is lost; but it is not too late to repair this condition.

To achieve the necessary definition of zones, the merely legal procedures of a zoning ordinance are not sufficient. It is necessary that each zone should be progressively replanned, as occasions present themselves, so as to achieve with greatest economy its special functions. Here the backwardness of street platting in Honolulu is a distinct advantage: it opens the way for more modern types. The great factories in the industrial zone, though perhaps they do not represent the highest degree of planning skill now available, are much more satisfactorily arranged for industrial purposes than if they had been put up on a uniform block system, designed to create the maximum number of building lots. The obstacles toward comprehensive planning in the business district are much more serious: but they should not result in an apathetic acceptance of the present inefficient layout. One of the first steps that suggests itself is the widening and planting of the mauka end of Bishop Street, the provision of a well-designed parking area, and the wiping away of the miscellaneous collection of buildings that spoils the magnificent vista toward the mountains. This whole process would be a relatively inexpensive one: yet overnight it would turn Bishop Street into one of the most attractive thoroughfares of its kind in the world: not merely more beautiful but vastly more efficient than the present jumble.

In the definition of zones, moreover, the use of parks and parkways should be considered, to give a visible frame to the zone or the neighborhood. A greenbelt or a park girdle, as little as a hundred feet wide, can give as much coherence to a modern neighborhood as the ancient wall used to do for the medieval city. Now it happens that the natural course of the original brooks and streams in the city, as well as most of the new drainage canals, is such as to check partly the otherwise uniform tendency to spread on either side of the original port. By utilizing such divisions, the city has the opportunity not merely to define the various natural neighborhoods of the city, but to open up, by means of the canal itself, its connections with the sea. Strips of water and strips of park, such as those by which the Ala Wai approaches the sea, would not merely increase the recreation zones of the city but give definition and order to its several parts. In this respect, Honolulu has a natural opportunity for a sound kind of planning that surpasses the opportunities of which the Dutch made such good use.

I have kept to the last the major weakness in Honolulu's development, although it has been touched on in relation to other matters. This is the low standard of housing and of open spaces that obtains in many portions of the city: not alone in the slums. The slums themselves are among the filthiest, the most overcrowded, and the most degraded in the world: that they are not even viler, when the physical conditions of life are considered, is a tribute to the personalities of their inhabitants. The overcrowding of the land in the central areas imposes upon a park program a burden that park planning by itself cannot relieve. Such an acute maldistribution of population may be beyond the physical powers of a Park Board effectually to correct. It creates a demand for open spaces precisely in those parts of the city where the land costs are highest, the land itself is hardest to acquire. These conditions throw a double burden on the community: first in the evils that derive directly from it, and second in the excessive cost of correcting them. Slum clearance and good low-cost housing become, therefore, more than an incidental part of a unified program of park development.

4. THE PERIOD OF EXPANSION IS PAST

Park Planning today is part of the broader process of ordering the human environment in such a way as to make the most of its varied possibilities. No park program can be permanently satisfactory until its policies and its plans are fitted into the general frame of the city's development, and represent the best thought available as to its development as a whole.

All intelligent planning today must begin with the recognition that the population of the United States is fast approaching a state of stability. Between 1945 and 1965 the normal increase in population through the excess of births over deaths will come to an end. This is not solely a big-city phenomenon, although the tendency shows itself most sharply in metropolitan areas: the same general facts apply even to relatively primitive areas like Oregon and Washington, where half the population is occupied on the farm or in the forest. These states have already apparently reached stability —a fact concealed only by the annual immigration from the dustbowl and other marginal agricultural areas. In many cases it will turn out that the earlier rather than the later date will hold.

Many people in Honolulu apparently believe that these islands are an exception to the general rule, because of the racial composition of the population. I have not had access to the most recent statistical analysis of this problem; but the sudden fall of the Japanese birth rate here, amounting to about twenty per thousand in a dozen years, would indicate that the same forces exist here as elsewhere, and may indeed manifest themselves, because of restricted economic opportunities, at an accelerated rate. Others, again, apparently hold that the present curve of population growth, which shows a decisive drop since 1930, is solely due to the economic crisis through which we have passed. A group of reputable engineers, who were giving counsel on an important public project, showed me the graph upon which they based their views of future needs. It showed a sharp upward increase in population up to 1930: at that point the curve flattened out: then, with 1938, it showed a continuation of the sharp original upward curve. If the depression were the sole cause of this flattening-out process, the upward movement should have been visible before 1938; but it did not in fact show itself, nor is there any special ground for believing that the present economic crisis is not a chronic one, attended by continued insecurity, fear, threats of war, and their deterrent effect upon the birth rate.

The depression is only one item in the present picture; the increase of cheap contraceptives and the extension of scientific contraceptive knowledge has more or less accompanied it. The general decline in population increase set in in England, for example, as early as 1870: by now it is almost a world-wide phenomenon, which would be even more conspicuous than it is already were it not for the fact that sanitation and public hygiene and medicine have lowered the number of deaths per thousand and increased the expectation of life.

We must accept the fact, then, that the great period of population expansion, which set in with the nineteenth century, is now drawing to a close. The National Resources Committee's Report on Cities, put the year when the population shall have ceased to increase as 1955: other estimates place it earlier. Meanwhile, the rate is rapidly dropping. Unless some profound change takes place, making parenthood as such more desirable and more attractive than it now is to the average married pair, population will be on a replacement basis.* In Hawaii, immigration from the mainland may for a while postpone the stabilization, particularly among the haole groups; but these are just the groups that show the steadiest decrease. All our activities must be reappraised with this fact in view. Instead of accepting quanti-

* Under pressure of catastrophe that change seems now taking place: at least the need for it and the conditions favoring it have appeared.

tative increase as no less desirable than inevitable, we must concern ourselves with qualitative development: we must bring into existence an environment that shall be favorable to the propagation and nurture of children, if only to maintain adequately the numbers we are now reduced to. And instead of making grandiose calculations as to future needs, whose over-optimism used to be automatically corrected by the mere flooding in of new members of the community, we must now make closer calculations. The pressure of population is now easing up: makeshift planning, jerry-building, amateurish improvisation, if they once had perhaps a colorable excuse for existence, no longer have any.

Most of the city plans, zoning schemes and road-building activities of the last two decades in America have ignored this approaching change. They still clung to the original notion, valid during the nineteenth century, that the population would continue indefinitely to expand and that the only thing that might hold this back would be lack of suitable mechanical facilities. Many cities of 300,000 during the past twenty years projected plans for absorbing populations as great as three million; and correspondingly reckless fantasies were accepted by allegedly sober bankers and investors as a basis for their financial calculations. It would have been bad enough if these projects had been merely committed to paper and placed on file in the municipal archives: unfortunately suburban subdivisions, street extensions, sewer and water main extensions were often put through far in advance of their actual use: similarly vast railroad stations, like that at Thirtieth Street in Philadelphia, were brought into existence to take care of an anticipated demand which was, in fact, diminishing. As a result of this overexpansion, cities throughout America have been decaying in their old centers, and over-extending themselves in raggedy fragments, often tax-delinquent or otherwise approaching private and public bankruptcy at the edges. Honolulu is not without examples of over-extension: consider St. Louis Heights. In many cases, the areas zoned for business and industry are from five to fifteen times the amount that any city would normally have used, even if the process of population increase had continued. Today these overblown attempts at civic greatness have become the signs of municipal bankruptcy. Planning for indefinite expansion is now wasteful and obsolete. The city of the future will have a better sense of its natural limits: it will attempt to make the most of what it has, rather than to evade its actual difficulties and its actual deterioration by encouraging its population to move out to the outskirts and permit the interiors to become more completely blighted. Good planning means rehabilitation: it means beginning over again and doing the job right.

The fact that Honolulu did not, before 1920, subject itself to plans of expansion is today one of its largest assets. Its central commercial and industrial areas are not very much larger than will satisfy its legitimate demands, although the infiltration of industries into areas from which they should be excluded must be watched with care. But, thanks to the approaching stability of population, Honolulu may at last pull itself together and create a permanent framework for its activities. With the approaching stability of population comes another possibility that has usually been foreign to our American city economy: the notion of permanence, particularly permanence in location and in the type of use to which a district or a zone is dedicated. Hitherto the exploitation of land has been on the assumption that the population would automatically increase: this increase in population would cause a rise in land values: the rise in land values in turn would cause a more intensive type of exploitation and would thus promote a change in use from residential to commercial, from low buildings to high buildings. From the standpoint of the land-owner or the real-estate speculator, this transformation was the main purpose of city development: no effort that promoted it was unworthy. Hence the popular programs for "attracting population."

Under such a system effective zoning was impossible, and effective planning, in which the street pattern could be adapted to the particular function served, was hopeless. Every street was planned to serve eventually as a through traffic artery; and blocks were laid out and land subdivided so as to produce the maximum number of saleable lots and street frontages, not so as to make the most economic and socially advantageous use of the site. With the diminishing pressure of population, there is a reasonable prospect of planning for permanent functions and permanent uses: not for the next few years alone, but at least for the next few generations. Planning that is done now will set the mold of the future. Hence it is important, both in the general scheme of planning and in each individual task, to take all the necessary time and forethought and technical skill and art that are necessary to effect a good plan.

Planning today works with a greater number of known factors than in the nineteenth century; and it can work toward a more definite social objective. As the pressure of population decreases, the pressure to get work done at once, before sufficient study has been made, before it fits into the general scheme of development, before it has been thought through to the point of complete integration, should be resisted. The acceptance on the part of the citizens of Honolulu—and even on the part of members of the Park Board—of such an irresponsible and random piece of planning as the bridge over the Ala Wai is almost as amazing as the project itself: the obstinate refusal to consider the bridge in relation to the present and future needs of Honolulu, exhibited by the Territorial Engineer, was as bad from the standpoint of method as from that of result. For good planning, today more than ever, is not a matter of putting through an isolated project: it is above all a matter of co-ordination. Planning that is thoroughly thought out and co-ordinated with other needs is necessarily slower than planning in a piecemeal and hit-or-miss fashion as opportunity hastily dictates: but that is no objection to it. If the pressure of population is over, the rush is over too.

5. FROM PRODUCTIVE OPPORTUNITIES TO CONSUMPTIVE DEMANDS

Still another conclusion follows from the approaching stability of population. During a period of expansion it was natural that industry should have the primary task of feeding the hungry mouths, clothing the naked bodies, linking together by railroad and steamship the newly settled areas. Hence new productive enterprises absorbed most of the available capital. By now, however, a great series of major industries have been built up and a vast productive plant is in existence. Although opportunities for new enterprises and new types of industrial goods will doubtless multiply, it should be plain that for the major industries the plants themselves will be on a replacement basis, and in the case of many commodities, the commodity itself will be on the same footing. Only one real field of expansion remains: that of raising the standard of living, of multiplying per person the amount of goods consumed. Whereas the emphasis in the nineteenth century was mainly on the fascinating new problems of production and transportation, the emphasis for the twentieth century must be on the no less urgent problems of distribution and consumption.

Many people are willing to acknowledge this approaching change; but they conceive it too much as taking place on the terms dictated by the past: namely, by a mere raising of the wage level and by a continued dependence upon individual consumer's demand, more or less manipulated—like the current demand for radios and motor cars—by the astute salesmanship of industries whose products lend themselves to fashion. Those who believe this overlook another kind of change that is taking place: a change in the mechanism of demand. Under the earlier economy, the demand of the individual consumer was for such goods as he could personally consume: this was the main regulator of production. To multiply and vary these individual needs seemed to the orthodox economist and the businessman the only basis for production: expanding individual wants meant an expanding market. Under this system, working-class families that failed to nourish their children properly might nevertheless possess a motor car; or they might live in a shabby, insanitary dwelling and still be tempted to purchase a suite of furniture far beyond their means.*

During the last generation, however, there has been a steady shift from individual demands, satisfied mainly by machine industry as an incident in the creation of profits and dividends, to collective demands, expressed in goods and services that are supplied by the community to all its citizens. What are called "perquisites" under the plantation system come to occupy a larger and larger place in a community's budget, when any attempt is made to normalize demands and to satisfy human needs, not by obeying solely the individual's caprice, but by taking care that the most important wants

* See the evidence set forth by Robert and Helen Lynd in Middletown.

should be met, whether the individual's own preference is sound or not. In urban communities we do not leave the provision of a sanitary water system or the provision of education to accidental choice: we erect a standard of cleanliness or of literacy and make acceptance obligatory to the whole community. "Perquisites" have become an important part in the community's budget: an increasing part of the annual income of the country goes to their provision. This shift in the incidence of demand gives to programs of city development and of housing a place of peculiar importance in the national economy: sound planning along these lines ensures that the shift in the distribution of income, which is inevitable if our productive system is to be kept running at all, shall be soundly managed, in such a fashion as to increase the real goods, in health, comfort, and joy, available to the ordinary citizen.

Education, recreation, hospital services, public hygiene have increased in importance in the national economy: they represent a collective need whose fulfillment the community cannot leave to the working out of the laws of supply and demand on the part of sporadic individuals. And just as the lessening of the number of workers needed in agriculture and primary industrial production shifts over to the administrative and professional services larger numbers of people, so the slackening of industrial expansion tends to thrust the surplus capital, not into new productive enterprise of a profit-making nature, but into those consumptive and cultural activities from which no immediate financial return can be expected, although each year may bring steady dividends in terms of intelligence, health, and spiritual animation. Such wealth, though apparently put to extravagant use, has the special virtue of not being readily consumed: and in that sense the cathedrals of the Middle Ages, for example, have

paid a return incomparably higher than the more profit-
making enterprises whose buildings and ships have long ago
rotted away.

Within the field of cities a similar shift can be detected.
The annual budgets of American cities show a decrease in
the amounts spent for streets, transportation, and other utilitarian operations as against the amounts spent upon health,
education, and recreation. This change expresses a real rise
in the standard of living, not merely as regards the quantity
of goods which the individual acquires, but still more with
respect to the quality. These new goods represent not the
means of living but living itself: the deepening of intelligence through study and research, the discipline of the emotions through music and the dance and the theater, the gain
in physical exuberance through swimming or tennis playing
or golfing in a beautiful environment.

Expenditures on these new items in the municipal budgets
have gained wide public approval: they represent an individual demand which the unaided individual is quite unable
to make economically effective. The increasing part played
by these collective utilities of culture is due to the fact that
goods which were once—like parks themselves—considered
the luxuries of a ruling minority have now become the necessities of daily life for the mass of the population. This
change represents, not the passing caprice of fashion, but a
profound re-orientation of life: it comes about as the result
of high taste and intelligence. Such collective consumption
is a true index of the culture of a country. In general, one
may look to relatively less capital going into profitable productive enterprise and more going into permanent civic
goods: one may look for a narrowing of individual demands
and toward greater opportunities for collective enjoyments
and satisfactions. Instead of an automatic expansion of the

productive mechanism, one may count upon a steady expansion of the consumptive mechanism, as population approaches stability.

This new field for expanded effort is a very large one. Few cities can boast that they have the accommodations they need for parks, playgrounds, schools, and museums on the scale that would be necessary if anything like a full quota of the population had the means to take advantage of them. In comparison with the abundant energies of our civilization, to say nothing of its superb technical equipment, the majority of our cities are in a state of pitiful impoverishment, filled with obsolete structures and makeshift urban services. The ugliness and sordid disarray of the usual American city, the existence of slums, the absence of a consistent and harmonious design in so much as a single quarter of the city, the failure to achieve a coherent pattern—all these things are a contradiction to the high pretensions of our civilization.

6. CAN CITIES HOLD THEIR POPULATION?

Before closing the subject opened by the approaching stability of population, one further consequence must be noted. The growth of the city in the past was dependent mainly upon its ability to draw newcomers from the once inexhaustible reserves in the open country. Although in general the diminution of the rate of increase is slower in rural areas than in cities, the same tendency is at work there: the supply is diminishing. Now it happens that most cities above twenty-five thousand in population do not reproduce their own numbers: without constant recruitment the city would diminish in population. This is true, even apart from the tendency on the part of many people to escape from the more congested and sordid internal sections of the city to outlying urban developments where at least a little sunlight, fresh air, and free play space can be secured for their children.

If these tendencies continue, the cities that now exist will be emptied out in their central areas, leaving a mass of rotting or dilapidated structures and a vast burden in capital investments whose returns are annually becoming smaller and shakier to the point of eventual tax delinquency and forfeiture. This has already happened on a vast scale on the mainland; and if the tendency is not so conspicuous as yet in Honolulu, it is something that must nevertheless be taken into account and guarded against. Under these conditions, the prime question of municipal policy becomes, not how the city is to expand and increase in population, but how it is to retain the population which the existing municipal utilities and the existing commercial enterprises have been framed to serve.

This question, I submit, can be successfully answered only if it is recognized that the older cities must be made over into sound biological environments. Cities that do not reproduce their population lack some necessary conditions for effective family life: high ground rentals, congestion, lack of play facilities, the threat of moral debasement, the uncertainties of economic existence—all these probably play a substantial part in shaping that multitude of individual decisions whose final result is the lowering of the birth rate.

If the existing city is not to go downhill in population, it must make itself over into the sort of environment in which having children will not be a burdensome liability. This calls for the systematic improvement of housing, the prevention of overcrowding, the establishment of standards of density of occupation, the creation of necessary public open spaces. Such measures should be framed and applied to all undeveloped areas at once, to keep them from turning into slums

and blighted districts: it calls likewise for their early application to older parts of the city, and in particular to those
ripe for demolition as pestilential slums. Finally, it calls for
the provision of gardens, parks, and recreation grounds on a
scale that will give to the city all the advantages that the
suburb usually has at the beginning of its existence—before
the suburb itself becomes a prey to speculative disorder and
congestion.

Ultimately, every well-administered municipality, in order
to save itself from bankruptcy and hopeless arrears, must
offset the tendency toward suburban growth by taking substantial measures toward its own renovation. *Not merely
must the municipality discourage such uneconomic growth
by resisting premature subdivision, by withholding assent
from ill-advised express highways, bridges, or tunnels that
open up cheap land outside the municipality's area of control: what is much more important is that it will seek to make
the city itself permanently attractive as a human home by
slum clearance, large-scale housing, neighborhood planning,
and park development. On any priority schedule for cities,
these things come first; and other municipal improvements
are acceptable only to the extent that they directly further
the movement toward urban rehabilitation.*

Pending the formulation and execution of such a comprehensive policy of city renewal, the city has the alternative
of accepting decay and paying a price for this decay in
deteriorated social and economic life. One large step toward
the formulation of a rational policy of city development,
however, can be made immediately through the provision of
park areas and playgrounds. Here the major outlines for a
long term development can be sketched out at once: the necessary land can be spotted and acquired; and a policy of

thorough systematic improvement, undertaken piecemeal, can be carried through over a long term of years. The strategic occupation of the open spaces of the city is the best guarantee of order and economy in the development of the building areas.

7. THE CHARACTER OF THE PRESENT PARK DEVELOPMENT

As with most American cities of the past, the city grew up without any systematic effort to conserve or bring into existence its needful open spaces. Nevertheless, though the development of Honolulu's parks was belated, the city already possesses the substantial framework of a comprehensive park system in the chain of parks that now begins with Ala Moana and passes along the shore area through Kapiolani Park and the intermittent connecting patches along Waikiki. These parks, together with the Ala Wai and the yacht basin at the end, transform the immediate neighborhood into what one may properly call the recreation zone of Honolulu.

But upon examining the recreational zone in connection with the population of the city as a whole, one is conscious of the fact that it does not extend far enough. The larger park areas are lopsidedly situated. The building of Ala Moana Park has partly served to rectify this condition; but as the sites for low-cost public housing, under the slum clearance program, are mainly on the Ewa side of the city, one may now raise the question as to whether there is not the possibility of a waterfront area in this section of the town that can be used by the nearby neighborhood communities. The lovely wooded island now occupied by the quarantine station cannot be left altogether out of such an inquiry; it might be that with a development of small ferries at various points, partly subsidized by the city, a very useful recre-

ational area could be made available. An early survey of
these various possibilities should be made.

The county park areas are admirably distributed around
the island, at least for all those forms of recreation that embrace the sea. But the use of these parks is for special occasions, such as holidays and weekends; and though they form
an essential part of any comprehensive scheme of recreation,
their existence does not diminish in the least the need for
day-to-day facilities that are accessible, without carfare, to
every family. It should not be forgotten that a fifteen cent
fare, though small to a middle-class purse, is an item that
must be reckoned with in the family budgets of the under-
privileged.

The total area dedicated to parks and playgrounds in
Honolulu comes to about one acre for 360 people; that of
city and country together to one for about 123 people. This
may seem a high standard in comparison with such space-
poor cities as New York; but in comparison with other American cities double Honolulu's size in population, it is relatively a low provision of open space. The deficiency is all
the more notable when one examines the apportionment of
parks by neighborhoods, because one discovers that in the
very areas where population is most clogged and where living conditions, from the point of view of health, are most
deplorable, the proportion of people to the acre of play
space is much higher.

The poor distribution of neighborhood playground space
is a sign of the fact that the park program has never been
treated as an integral part of the city's development. Random
pressures and opportunities have evidently controlled the
acquisition of land for park purposes: there has been no
systematic effort to relate the amount of space dedicated to
the social and hygienic needs of the inhabitants. Similar

pressures, moreover, have undoubtedly been responsible for the premature development of this tract or the tardy development of another. One group with an active neighborhood leader wants a playground and, because it is vocal and insistent, gets it; another group, in much more serious need, never makes its need visible or audible and is forgotten. Such haphazard planning, such indolent opportunism, are inevitable until a comprehensive and long-term plan for park development is instituted. Such a plan would have a definite priority schedule, based upon actual social need: its budgetary demands would be based upon these needs and distributed, where the expenditure involved was large, over a sufficiently long term of years; the Park Board would then be under no pressure to dribble away a few thousand dollars here because of special demands which should be met, if at all, in a later stage of its work. And without this plan, even the most efficient of boards must be the victim of mere opportunism: a policy that is economically wasteful and fatal to any orderly development.

Another weakness of a vague program of park development is that, with each area crying for special attention, with each recreation purpose demanding its special tribute, it is difficult to put through any single job systematically. One of the weaknesses in urban psychology is that the city man, in our day, has accustomed himself to dealing only in finished products, ignorant of the long period of growing and processing that must take place before the can or the package or the machine reaches him. Hence a certain impatience over the unfinished, based upon ignorance and the failure to understand nature's slow processes. While much can be done, perhaps, by way of public education to make the urban intelligence appreciate the need for time in perfecting a park or any other structure, it is advisable to meet the city man's im-

patience at least halfway. One of the reasons for Mr. Moses'
popularity as Park Commissioner in New York City is the
fact that, even with some initial extravagance, he concen-
trates his resources on a particular job and carries it through
till the improvement is finished. A scattering of half-developed
parks is not so impressive as one park that has been brought
to a state of completion. While such a development must not
sacrifice real efficiency to effect, the demonstrative value of
a perfected work, in arousing popular demand, must not be
overlooked.

No adequate park program for the city itself can be laid
down until certain necessary statistical information has been
collected. What is needed is a block-by-block canvass of
neighborhoods to establish the number of families, the number of people per block, the number of children, the age
distribution of all the people surveyed, and finally their
present recreational preferences. Such a survey could easily
have been included in the National Youth Survey done a
little while ago, had the need for it been formulated then:
part of the necessary data might possibly be included in the
Real Property Inventory, which has recently been projected
here, to be done with WPA money, on the general lines done
on the mainland. If this opportunity does not open up, I
suggest that samples be taken in various parts of the city;
and the results checked up for the neighborhood as a whole
with social workers, physicians, and other experienced observers working in the district.

The reason for such a survey becomes plain as soon as
one sets out the requirements of a broadly organized park
system, as contrasted with a mere collection of publicly
owned open spaces. As Olmsted pointed out two generations
ago, park areas should grade upward from the immediate
patch of open space around the individual house or group

of houses to the widest and most comprehensive regional recreational uses, drawing upon the inhabitants of many communities. The core of such a development is obviously the individual garden. Within the residential block there should be small enclosed play areas for the play of little children directly under the eyes of their mothers: a sand pile, a board, a few sturdy boxes are almost all that is needed by way of equipment. The proper design of residential blocks involves the correct placing and hedging of such a play area.

The next type of playground is that which should serve the group of families forming a neighborhood: a bigger play area for sports like tennis, basketball, or even baseball—or as an alternative, swimming. Here, again, small areas, sufficient for the play of children from four to twelve, should be more numerous than the bigger areas for children above that age and for adults: since the tolerable walking distance to a playground differs according to the age of the user; and whereas half a mile may not be too far for older children, it effectually excludes the younger group.

In addition to such active recreational areas, open greens and shaded promenades should be established in neighborhoods to serve as attractive places where the older members may meet, gossip, flirt, or court in accordance with their age, sex, and inclination. The courtship of boys and girls in the city's street, or in the drab places on the outskirts where they may take refuge for greater privacy, is one of the most pitiable spectacles that the modern city furnishes: it gives to all the amatory explorations of youth an air of furtiveness, sordidness, and shabbiness which subtly corrodes the entire sexual life. One of the best uses to which any park may be put is obviously to serve as a harmonious meeting place for young lovers: the prolongation and enrichment of courtship

is one of the best ways to intensify sexual ardor and forfend
boredom.

We should not forget that in the Western world the planning of parks and the introduction of courtship as an erotic
ritual came in together in the royal courts, as the very word
courtship indicates; and it is high time that a little public
wisdom was applied to this area of life. If wiping out sexual
disease is an imperative hygienic matter, building up a rich
and many-sided culture of sex is no less an important contribution to family well-being. I have been in public parks
on the mainland where motorcycle police with searchlights
obscenely blazed upon park benches in order to interrupt the
tender moments of lovers: a perversion far worse than the
loosest sexual abandon that the searchlight might discover.
Just the opposite of this is needed: public gardens and promenades that lovers will take to naturally, in preference to the
sordid quarters that dishonor their every emotion. Without
any ostentatious declaration of purpose, the placing and the
planting of neighborhood promenades may well make a positive contribution to the biological well-being of the community, through their direct effect upon the moods and feelings
of the young.

8. LOCAL GREENBELTS

One of the great principles established by modern urban
design is the necessity for greenbelts to give shape and coherence to the local community and to keep it from being
invaded, once its character is established, by a lower order
of urban building. The failure to establish a greenbelt at
Forest Hills, Long Island, for example, turned out to be a
miserable "economy": what it did was to invite the speculative builder to creep up to the very door of the community
and fatten himself on the values created by good planning,

whilst lowering the values of the neighboring property. The greenbelt serves a triple purpose, then: it gives a coherent pattern to the neighborhood; it prevents encroachment; it provides needed park space. Moreover, the provision of intra-urban parks in long strips has the excellent effect of spreading park services over a wider area; while, at the same time, it avoids the vice of parks like Central Park in New York of taking too large a chunk out of the urban building area and more or less blocking its articulated development.

Honolulu has the special advantage of having its greenbelt areas more or less provided by nature. On the mauka side, the spurs of the mountains that lead down into the city form natural open areas that can only be developed for urban building at an extravagant cost. Where these areas have not already been sacrificed to the subdivider, they should be retained and connected together as a greenbelt. Where the soil and rainfall lend themselves to further cultivation, these areas may be kept in active use as market gardens and fruit-tree plantations. Otherwise they should be left open for the occasional picnicker and excursionist.

Far more important than this mauka greenbelt is the opportunity offered by drainage canals. Much of the land upon which Honolulu was built in the past cannot effectively rid itself of surface water without an artificial drainage system. So far, these canals have been constructed mainly for the purely utilitarian purpose of getting rid of the water. The magnificent contribution made by the Ala Wai is to show that if the drainage canals are on an adequate scale, they may be combined in handsome fashion with park strips. These strips serve as green lanes that may define the boundaries of a neighborhood and provide a park vista toward the open sea. An incidental use of such canals is that they serve as positive barriers against fire. Nature has here given the city planner a potent ally—provided he has the imagination and the means to make use of it.

A system of drainage canals, bordered by parks, would give to Honolulu a special character like that which lends its charm to Annecy in the Alps. The fact that a new canal is now in course of building without any provision having been made for such park strips shows that the significance of the drainage canal from the planning standpoint has not been grasped either by the engineers of the city or, for that matter, by the Park Board itself. As far as the internal development of the parks of Honolulu goes, the working out of a park and drainage canal system for every great neighborhood area is perhaps the most important item to be added to the immediate program.

9. THE PLACE OF ARTERIAL PARKWAYS

If the bringing of the sea into the heart of Honolulu is one item in a complete park program, the bringing of the countryside into the system by means of at least two major parkways, running more or less parallel to the sea on the one hand and the base of the hills on the other, is equally important. The plotting out of such parkways, with roadways for travel in opposite directions separated by a green planted strip, would fill a double need: It would give Honolulu the fast and safe traffic artery that it needs, instead of the series of impediments and bottlenecks that now stand in the way of quick intercommunication; and it would link up the various park services more closely than is now possible. These parkways should skirt the makai and the mauka sides of Honolulu. Far from congesting traffic in a central point, their aim should be to pick it up and drop it at intervals all along the route.

Every alternative to this scheme goes against the fundamental principle of arterial planning: namely, it piles traffic upon streets that are already used and already over-burdened; and in order to achieve the necessary width for the arterial avenue, it is compelled to condemn and tear down large swathes of existing buildings. Moreover, the widening of any of the existing streets has the further dis-advantage of imposing a major financial burden upon the city and its property owners. Whereas arterial parkways, skirting the city at either side and leading out into the coun-try, would have a claim for Federal assistance.*

The reader will note that I speak not of arterial roads but of arterial *parkways*. Here is an important difference be-tween these two types of traffic arterial: the arterial road is a wide thoroughfare, almost impossible for the pedestrian to cross and extremely disagreeable to travel on because of the glare and the usual ugliness of the straggling business or residential developments on each side. A parkway, on the other hand, that has a right-of-way at least one hundred feet wide, can be planted so as to offer complete shade and cool-ness for those who drive along it, as well as a maximum degree of safety for those who wish to cross it.

Once such parkways were built and planted on a large scale, they might well influence the rebuilding of the com-mercial areas of the city. Here the narrow streets, and the unrestrained abandonment of shade trees on most of them, show a wanton neglect of a beautiful opportunity. The mer-chants' notion that the chopping down of shade trees on busi-ness thoroughfares is a sign of progress or business efficiency

---

* The failure to act on this proposal—whose military importance I stressed in private conference—was costly. I quote from a letter from Honolulu dated 20 March 1941: "Defense matters have so swamped Honolulu that the movement of traffic is something frightful. It often takes . . . as much as three-quarters of an hour for an automobile to travel through the business district of Honolulu."

is one of those blind superstitions that cannot be justified by sound business practice. Shopping along shaded streets, as every visitor to Paris knows, is a far more delightful pastime than shopping in the barren waste of an American commercial district. It is likely to take longer, too, and this is to the advantage of the shop keeper; whereas the open glare of the hot pavements often tempts the buyer to reduce as far as possible the time spent on shopping. Even the partial attempt to combine trees with buildings on Bishop Street is an excellent step. It gives one a hint of what the smaller thoroughfares in the city might be if the spirit of the park were brought, by means of a parkway, into the heart of the built-up quarters. The opportunity for adequate park treatment that was opened by the widening of River Street, as I must point out incidentally, has so far been neglected. This would be a proper starting point for making the tree-lined street a normal feature of all street widenings and straightenings in Honolulu.

10. NEW PARK AREAS

While, as I have pointed out, the broad outlines of a city and regional park system have been well laid down, there are a few links that remain to be connected. One of these is the extension of the Ala Moana-Waikiki ocean park development from Kahala up to Koko Head. The great reef outside the Kahala section obstructs the use of the waterfront there for either sailing or boating. By dredging part of the reef and using the material to fill in a strip on the ocean side, a new park and parkway could be created which would connect directly with the park already acquired at Hanauma Bay. At the same time it would provide an opportunity that Honolulu, for all its love of water sports, strangely lacks: that is, a large quiet area that can be used for diving and deep-water swimming.

One other weakness in the regional park system is the inadequate frontage the Park has acquired at Kailua. Here is an exceptionally fine natural beach—perhaps the best in the island. It answers, in fact, to what the traveler thinks of when he hears the name "Waikiki." But already a great part of this beach has been carelessly permitted to go into private ownership and to be built over. Meanwhile, land values have been going up, and if the Pali tunnel is put through, this part of the island will not be much more than twenty or twenty-five minutes away from the heart of Honolulu. It will, therefore, draw a load of Sunday visitors comparable to that of the most visited beaches within the city itself. Hence the need for acquiring a more sufficient park area here is highly urgent—so urgent, indeed, that I would suggest it be acquired by special funds, since the annual sum dedicated to the Park Board for the acquisition of new properties is plainly insufficient to acquire an adequate amount of land at an early enough date.

In looking over the various types of park, playground, and recreation area that the Park Board has developed, I am impressed by the wide variety of uses and by the wide range of interests that have been served. With the policy of devoting each of the great park areas to a more or less specialized purpose—using Kapiolani Park for horse riding and polo playing; the Ala Wai for boating and boat racing; and Ala Moana Park for tennis, bowls, and aquatic sports— I am in thorough agreement. It seems to me, however, that there are two special kinds of park that might well be added to the present system in order to embrace a fuller range of activities.

One kind of park that is lacking is the upland wild park:

the primeval park. Such a park should be located in the hills. It should include within a relatively narrow compass, perhaps, a wide range of topography and natural vegetation: There should be an example of semi-tropical jungle; there should be, if possible, one or more ti slides; there should be a stream and a waterfall of a kind that has always contributed to the traditional delights of Polynesian existence.* Such a park could have the barest minimum of physical equipment: at most, rough open shelters for overnight camping, simple stone fireplaces for cooking, and a mere clearance through the denser vegetation for the hiker and the picnicker. Contrary to the unwise practice of some of the large primeval parks and reservations on the mainland, access to such parks should not be made too easy. The roads leading to them should be planned to attract only those who wish the experience of roughness, of simplicity, and of solitude in the midst of Nature. This excludes large, well-surfaced roads and large parking areas that would attract the sort of picnicker whose very presence would rob the scene of the value it holds for those who meet its challenge.

On the windward side of the island, Dr. Nils Larsen has a tract of land which very closely meets the requirements that I have set down here, and it gives an opportunity for recreation of an entirely different kind from that suggested by the sunnier parts of the shore. I would suggest that a small area combining these advantages be set aside experimentally to determine whether the primeval park has as close an attraction for the Hawaiian citizen as it has for the inhabitant of the mainland.

* The primeval sport of dry-land coasting, seated on a broad ti leaf, is, like surf-riding, a breath-taking and dangerous performance: more so, perhaps, than the Polynesian sport of plunging down a waterfall. Like surf-riding, it is one of those daring activities by which aristocracies keep themselves in trim, alert to danger, ready for death.

While on the subject of the primeval park, I should like to
add one other thought to the development of the more aquatic
parks along the shore. The ocean, too, is part of our primeval
inheritance. The love of almost all the peoples in the Pacific
for the water is one of their most fundamental characteristics.
It unites the Hawaiian, the Samoan, the Filipino, and the
Japanese. Without any undue piety toward the now archaic
Hawaiian traditions, it seems to me that salt-water fish ponds,
constructed and stocked on traditional lines, might well be a
useful addition to the recreational opportunities of some of
the outlying parks.

I note that various proposals have been made to construct
a typical Hawaiian village in connection with one of the
parks within the city. This seems to me a highly inappropri-
ate urban enterprise but, on the other hand, it might well
be the crowning achievement in one of the wilder and more
distant areas that the Park Board has set aside for public
recreation. To come to such a village among its natural sur-
roundings, and to participate (up to a point) in some of the
typical recreational resources of the old Hawaiian village,
would be an excellent way of not merely recalling the past
but enriching the present.

One further point. One of the greatest delights of bathing
in the sea or the sun is the enjoyment of untrammeled contact with these elemental forces. They invite a certain ease,
a certain abandonment of the usual conventionalities of civilization: above all, the ancient convention of wearing clothes.
Every swimmer knows that nakedness gives the last touch to
his enjoyment of the water and that even the wearing of
trunks takes away a little of the edge of that pleasure. In
England, a country that invented Mrs. Grundy, there has
long been the custom, at various public bathing beaches, of
reserving certain hours when men could go into the water

without wearing clothes. Such segregated bathing shocks no
one and there is no reason why a similar convention should
not be established on one or more of the beaches of Oahu—
applying to women as well as to men. While this proposal
perhaps runs in the face of an ancient missionary tradition
in these islands, it is time to recognize that the shamefaced-
ness and the distrust of the body which the early missionaries
showed in their contact with Polynesian civilization no longer
represents the sanest thought of the community. Rather, one
detects in it a prurience and a libidinousness born of qualities the very opposite of those that they affected to promote.
To restore to both Hawaiian and haole alike the privilege
of confronting the primeval forces of the ocean and the sun
in Adam's original garb is but a just measure of restitution
for the restrictions and burdens imposed by what one of Herman Melville's characters derisively called "snivelization."

In extreme contrast to the primeval, wild park is another
type of park that represents the very apex of esthetic culture:
the formal garden. In the Banyan Garden in Ala Moana
Park, Honolulu has a brilliant example of such formal planning. As public funds become more available, the development of such gardens in other areas of the city would be
extremely desirable. They would form natural centers for
local dramatic activities, and they might well lend their
beauty to great formal occasions in life—like a wedding or
the celebration of the anniversary of a marriage, or the hon-
oring of some local public character. In providing such
formal gardens in future, I should expect to see a further
development in esthetic design that would make the garden
itself as conspicuous an example of modern taste and modern
Hawaiian traditions as the new buildings that have recently
been created, under the Park Board, in the Ala Moana Park
and other places.

But while favoring and emphasizing the utilization of contemporary motifs and materials in planting and garden architecture, as well as in building proper, it seems to me that there is room in Honolulu for at least one or two small examples of the high garden art of the Chinese and the Japanese. There are a number of private gardens around the city which exemplify the special characteristics of these cultures, but in a city where the Oriental races have contributed so much to the vividness and color of its life, some public recognition should be given to one of their supreme contributions to culture. Many Americans, unable to push beyond Hawaii, will get their first and only real contact with the older civilizations of the East through what evidences they find in these islands. For their sakes, as well as for the edification and delight of the permanent residents of Honolulu, one or two conspicuously good public examples of Japanese and Chinese gardening would be an asset for the city which might —even in dollars and cents—prove one of its most profitable investments. Were the desire for such a garden given public expression, it is even possible that some wealthy citizen, with a talent for philanthropy, would ensure the ultimate passage of his private garden into public possession.

11. DESIGN AND FUNCTION OF NEIGHBORHOOD PLAYGROUNDS

With respect to the provision of neighborhood playgrounds, I have already mentioned their weaknesses in number and placement. These weaknesses can be corrected only after making a systematic canvass of neighborhood needs. But I cannot leave this subject without saying a word as to the character of these developments: for from the standpoint of permanent economy, rational design, and esthetic mastery, the best playgrounds of Honolulu seem to me definitely su-

perior to those I have seen on the mainland, not excluding
some of the excellent ones that the Moses administration has
erected in New York, to say nothing of the well-established
structures of an older period in Chicago.

Too often playgrounds are regarded by municipal authorities as permanent waste-spaces—or unoccupied lots—set
aside for play. That the very spirit of play is enhanced by
taking place in a setting that shows order and vision often
does not occur to the municipal departments concerned:
hence ugly chicken-wire fences, clay or bare asphalt sur-
faces, and a complete innocence of all esthetic device. Honolulu has made a valuable departure from this stale tradition
by providing, in some of its new playgrounds, structures that
have none of this tawdry makeshift quality: they are rather
examples of building art worthy to have a place beside the
open-air gymnasiums or palestra of the Greeks. The handsome bounding wall, the judicious planting of shade trees,
the retention of grass wherever possible, translate the spirit
of organized play to the area itself.

This tradition should take permanent root in Honolulu:
the spirit called forth in the Mother Waldron Playground
should be infused into all the city's playground activities.
But one important opportunity should not be missed: that of
co-ordinating school-building with playground-building, and
vice versa. Here an administrative unification is necessary,
to the effect that the Park Board should design and administer all the playgrounds of the city, including those attached
to public schools, so that these areas themselves should have
the highest competence brought to their design and should
be used to the greatest extent possible. If in the new housing
units that may be put up in future by either the Hawaiian
Housing Authority or the city itself, playgrounds are pro-

vided as part of the original design, the Park Board should be brought in and the supervision and upkeep of the new area should be placed under the Board's jurisdiction. All this will doubtless add to the burdens of the Board and call for both a larger staff and a larger share of the city's annual income. But the present division of responsibility here is wasteful; and it works against the building up of a comprehensive park system.

There are park properties, insignificant in extent and improperly located, that might well be traded off or sold in order to acquire land in more appropriate areas. It would need a more thorough study than I have had the opportunity to make to suggest precisely where such land should be acquired; but an obvious place to begin is in connection with the razing of congested slums. In some cases the sites so cleared may be better adapted to park purposes than to any other uses.

Along these lines I have one further suggestion to make. In the older type of city planning the park formed an isolated open area in the midst of a pattern of built-up blocks. In the new type of city planning, with the development of superblocks and closed cul-de-sacs, treated as more or less self-contained areas for domestic services, the neighborhood ribbon park becomes the very core of effective design. It is the natural site for the elementary school and, in general, it makes it possible for the child to walk to and from school without crossing a traffic street. This gives the school itself the quiet and isolation necessary for good classroom work, and it brings the park itself closer to the door of the individual home. Such a design, once worked out successfully, should have a potent effect upon the laying out of new residence areas in all the islands, possibly even on the West Coast: quite as potent an effect as Radburn has had in the

East, or as Frankfurt-am-Main had throughout Europe before 1932.

This brings up one further point: the close connection between a sound park policy and a program for rehousing the occupants of decayed and congested areas. The rational control of land use, with respect to density of occupation and open spaces, is an indispensable part of any valid park system. Through the creation of parks, the city establishes a proportion of open land to occupied land for the city as a whole. This, however, is only a part of a well-oriented program. Such a standard of open spaces and density must be established for every area. There are slums in Honolulu that are so congested that adequate park space for the existing population would cover a larger area than is devoted to the building themselves. Such a condition is intolerable: and it is incurable by any one-sided effort of the Park Board, no matter how vast the means that might be placed at its disposal. In England, the vast re-housing developments of the last twenty years have been at average densities of twelve or less families per acre. Such a standard implies reasonable land values, and in turn it guarantees that such values will remain reasonable.

Under the police powers, the American city has ample constitutional means for controlling the density of population and extent of land coverage in the interest of public health and hygiene. Before these standards can be established and protected by law, however, the city will have to tackle a much more difficult problem: that of opening up the major land areas within the city for orderly human occupation. There can be no sound or effective planning of either neighborhoods or parks and playgrounds so long as land values here remain prohibitively high. High land values mean high rents: these conditions in turn place a premium upon congestion and upon bad types of architectural design.

This problem came down to the present-day city out of special historical conditions with which everyone in Honolulu is familiar. With the right and wrongs of these conditions, the city planner need have no concern: but about the urgency of correcting them he must speak in no uncertain terms. All available legal means should be taken at once to reduce land values to a saner level. By opening up for public housing territorially owned land on the outskirts of the city, by using the process of eminent domain to take over for public purposes land held against public interest out of use, by establishing low maximum densities of population per acre for all new developments, by enforcing the minimum standards of hygiene and sanitation in now overcrowded quarters—by these means a vigilant planning authority would correct the inherent evils of a short-sighted monopoly. And without such comprehensive aid, the Park Board can scarcely hope to catch up with actual needs or provide anything like the full services and facilities a modern city should demand.

Park planning, in other words, cannot possibly stop at the edges of the parks: its greatest need is to infuse its standards of space and beauty and order into every other aspect of the city's developments. The park system is thus the very spearhead of comprehensive urban planning.

12. THE QUALITY OF DESIGN IN PARKS

Parks have been called the lungs and the breathing spaces of the city; and this important aspect of the park has perhaps tended to obscure the fact that they are, in reality, much more than that. An empty lot is also an open space, but no matter how big it is, it is not a park until it has been adapted

to the special civic needs that a park fulfills. The origin of
all municipal parks is the royal park, like the Tuileries or
St. James's Park: the outdoor part of the palace. The quality
of design, which marked the architecture of the palace, likewise infused itself into the park: in making a setting for
promenades and play, a certain amount of formalization
necessarily enters into the conception of the park. Sometimes
the deliberate parts of the design are elaborately concealed
by naturalistic artifice, as in the great romantic parks designed during the nineteenth century by Frederick Law Olmsted, an American of world-wide renown; but even in the
most pastoral and informal settings, Olmsted's esthetic touch
was everywhere visible; and in the most successful landscape
park of all, the Prospect Park in Brooklyn, Olmsted provided
for strongly formalized entrances, even as (with Vaux) in
the design for Central Park the plan of the Mall and the
great stairs and esplanade that lead down to the water, he
did not hesitate to depart from "free" design into the strictest
kind of order.

In remoter portions of a region, where the natural landscape is of too striking a character to be modified by the
works of man, nature may well be left in her savage state:
but to achieve success here, it is important that access to
the spot should not be too easy and the opportunities for
recreation should remain of the most primitive character.
In park developments where this has not been observed, as
for example on Mount Rainier in Washington, with its ten
thousand visitors on a single day, the very feeling of primeval mountain masses and untrammeled spaces and terrifying
heights is badly spoiled by the suburban nature of all the
vast facilities that care for and feed the curious visitor.

On the more striking beaches, like that by Koko Head,
very little in the way of design need be added to nature's

achievements. But where crowds of people are going to gather for essentially social pleasures, design is an essential part of the whole park relationship. The people's park, no less than the royal park, should convey a certain sense of order and by the planting of every tree, the design of every building, give a sense of what life's environment may be at its best: spacious, harmonious, rhythmic, infused with that quality of keen vitality for which the names "art" and "beauty" must serve as commonplace equivalents. Esthetic delight is not something that should be segregated for the connoisseur of pictures or statues: not an emotion that one puts on tap on entering a museum and forgets in daily life. It is the natural reaction of the common man when the sea is blue and the sky dazzling, when a water lily unfolds in a pond, when a clean, finely proportioned building extends its welcome to him when he enters it. No amount of attention that is paid to the esthetic part of park design is wasted, for beauty is the best preservative of a park or a building. An ugly, disheveled environment discourages good use: whereas a handsome, well-ordered environment usually stimulates the best kind of human reaction: under normal circumstances people take personal pride in maintaining such beauty.*

The formal beauty of good architectural design and the spirit of play are indeed closely akin: where, indeed, is there a finer rhythm or a keener sense of design in space than in the balance of a surf-rider's body, in the delivery of a fine serve in tennis, or the curve of a diver's body as he leaps from the diving board? Beauty of form in sport is not obtained by accident: it is obtained by practice, by emulation,

---

* No one who has participated in the spontaneous ritual of observing the opening of the night-blooming cereus on the walls around the Punahou School will ever forget either the sense of almost religious reverence or the esthetic awe of such a moment. Such collective rituals might be multiplied.

by the deliberate exercise of human skill. It is this sort of
beauty that counts in the design of parks; and it is by no
means an accident, perhaps, that possibly the most delightful
playground for the young of all ages in the world, the Jardin
du Luxembourg, is within the compass of a highly formalized
park and garden.

In park planning, as in every other department of civic
economy, the wise counsel is that of Emerson's: save on the
low levels and spend on the high ones. It is poor economy
to erect makeshift structures that will presently look stale
and seedy, will rot or lose their coat of paint, and will either
have to be replaced or form a permanent eyesore. It is real
economy to build whatever structures are really needed in
durable and handsome materials, whose annual upkeep is
low, and whose life may be measured in decades and centuries, rather than years. For of all the parts of a city in
which permanence may be expected, its parks rate highest;
and that fact should be taken advantage of in the design
of its structures. Simple, straightforward designs, carried
through with an eye mainly to proportions, texture, and
color, have a power to outlast all the minor changes of convention and taste. Mechanical equipment, on the other hand,
is subject to rapid obsolescence: hence this item should be
reduced to the lowest amount compatible with convenience
and sound upkeep. Premature expenditures on half-baked
developments are wasteful. It is better to go slowly with the
development of parks, until the need for larger amounts of
the annual municipal budget is recognized, than to undertake makeshift improvements whose main feature is the fact
that they will have to be remade. With the growth and more
intensive use of the parks, the amount of funds allocated
to park work should, it goes without saying, be proportion-

ately increased. Until that demand is recognized and cordially met, a slow development of the existing properties seems to me the only prudent course.

Although all the main parks under the Park Board are in an incomplete state, the quality of their design is evident. Especially to be commended is the use of the native tropical vegetation to the greatest extent possible, and the handsome, clear-cut character of all the new structures. The architectural treatment of Ala Moana Park and the design of the Mother Waldron Playground seem to me particularly successful: these have their parallel in the handsome bathing structure and pergola in the coastal park at Waialua. The Park Pavilion in Ala Moana, giving on to the beautiful formal garden and pool, will, if developed according to the original plan of serving as restaurant, provide a setting that is equaled in few places in the world. The closest approach to this possibility is in the handsome restaurant that has been built, under the commissionership of Robert Moses, in the Central Park Zoo in New York. The great merit, indeed, of all of Mr. Moses' park developments, from the magnificent seaside park at Jones Beach to his smallest municipal playground, is that every spot that his architects and planners touched bears the mark of highly rational purpose, intelligible design, and esthetic form. No spot is too mean, no function is too humble to exist without benefit of art. It is useless to seek in the past of Hawaii or any other region the esthetic precedent for the new structures that the urban parks need. That will have to be found, through continued experiment, in the line already established by the boathouse on the Ala Wai and the other buildings I have mentioned. In landscape design, and in the working out of formal gardens, further thought and imagination are needed: but the architectural precedent is by now well established, and the

need for an architectural form, clean, vivid, strong enough
to hold its own against the effects of sea and mountain,
should be obvious.

13. MEANS OF WORKING OUT A PROGRAM

As far as technical assistance is concerned, the parks have,
during the last few years, been very fortunate. The character
of the design has been thoroughly in harmony with regional
needs, without any attempt to reproduce archaic patterns or
to draw upon foreign historic sources. Under the priority
schedule that has apparently existed in the minds of at least
the Chairman of the Board and its Architect, the most important elements have been put first and nothing has been
scamped in order to give the work as a whole the appearance
of being finished before it actually was ready to be done
effectively.

But park planning, from the very nature of things, touches
every other aspect of the city's existence. The quality of
space, which is a matter essential to urban health and beauty,
is a quality that comes especially within the province of the
Park Department. Spacing is no less essential an element
than placing and building—just as in music the interval may
be as important for the musical effect as the notes that are
actually struck. But it is obvious that the work of preparing
and executing a comprehensive park program for Honolulu
must, under the present political arrangements, be an obstacle race for even the most earnest and intelligent and
civic-minded board. Planning involves relationship and the
parks for Honolulu cannot be planned in correct relationship
to all its other urban and industrial needs unless some authority is actively dealing with these things and formulating
a rational treatment for them. Even the present park program
has been seriously handicapped by the lack of any authorita-

tive planning commission in the city capable of formulating and carrying out a co-ordinated program of city development.

Now the City Planning Commission has been in existence for seventeen years. During that time it has, no doubt, accomplished a great deal of useful pedestrian work, but because of lack of active public support, lack of intelligent co-operation on the part of elected officials, and perhaps also lack of sufficiently imaginative leadership, it has so far done little to anticipate the major constructive enterprises upon which the city must embark. In view of the circumstances under which it has functioned, no blame attaches to the City Planning Commission for this failure. Lack of political authority and lack of financial support have hamstrung even its most modest efforts. Such a commission might be composed of Michelangelos and Haussmanns without being able to add an iota to its present performance. Unfortunately, half-hearted city planning is in some ways worse than no city planning at all, for it gives the impression that some provision has been made, that some work is being done, that some careful eye is overseeing all the city's developments. Whereas in reality, habit and routine continue to throttle every attempt to improve the city's present condition.

For the sake of doing its own work more effectively, the Park Board must necessarily interest itself in the better composition of the city government, must concern itself, in other words, with the very important political and administrative revisions that the present Charter Committee must undertake to incorporate in their recommendations.

The first important need for a new type of city planning authority is to break through the water-tight compartments in which the various city departments now work. Departmental jealousy is an obvious and ever-present cause for the failure to work out a common solution of a common problem, and one of the causes for this jealousy is mere ignorance of what the other departments are doing, while another is the desire to acquire for one's own department as large a share as possible of the municipal budget. This rivalry is, of course, not peculiar to city officials and certainly not peculiar to Honolulu. One may observe exactly the same friction at work in the administration of any university. While relatively, administrative autonomy is one of the secrets of responsibility and efficiency in any organization, such autonomy cannot exclude the need for common plans and for common means of effecting those plans. Indeed, certain matters which concern other city departments and functions should be made mandatory for common consultation and common action.

The recent case of the Ala Wai bridge crystallizes the dangers that are inherent in the present scheme. The engineer of a territorial public works board chose to consider the bridge as an independent, self-sustaining structure. His plan of the bridge was prepared without the slightest real consideration for the park approach, for the yacht basin approach, for the safety of the pedestrians having to cross the Ala Moana Boulevard, or for the probable need of a much broader parkway.* But the fact is that a bridge can have no such independent existence. Whether it is a good bridge or a bad one does not depend merely upon its structural efficiency but upon its ability to work in harmoniously with the other needs of the area it serves. To plan, design, or build such a bridge except as part of an authorized city planning scheme, duly examined and thoroughly criticized by the authorities concerned, is not merely shortsighted but extremely wasteful. Such unco-ordinated building has characterized a good part of the conventional improvements that

---

* All this was fully confirmed after the bridge was built.

have been made by urban authorities throughout the country.

Another example, almost comic in its ineptitude, recently occurred in Honolulu, in which a recently paved street was torn up within a few months of the completion of the paving job, in order to lay down water pipes. Still another example of this mischievous isolation that now exists between city departments is the proposed new street that is to be carried over the Ala Wai. The basis upon which this short-cut from the hills to Waikiki is urged is an obsolete one: it would sacrifice the unity and beauty of one of Honolulu's proudest city planning developments (namely, the Ala Wai itself) in order to cut a minute or two of traveling time between two sections of the city that, on the basis of their prospective population or prospective amount of social intercourse, have no need of any such rapidity of movement.

Whereas intelligent city planning is always concerned to reduce the number of streets to the lowest possible level, half-baked city planning, lacking in sound social objective, usually distinguishes itself by adding streets and traffic thoroughfares to areas where they are not needed. The cure for such erratic projects lies not so much in a master plan by itself as in a master policy: a program of civic action, formulated by minds that are capable of holding in view the good of the city as a whole and who are not afraid to go contrary to prevailing practices when those practices have proved to be obsolete and inefficient and wasteful.

How is the necessary city planning program to be achieved? How is the city planning education of the citizens and the professional groups of Honolulu to be extended? How is a coherent master plan to be formulated, not as an arbitrary exercise of technical authority but as a resolute consensus of the city's best intelligence about its needs and its possibilities of future development?

Informal co-operation between various departments and groups may prove very useful as a first step, but some more systematic and inevitable method of obtaining a common approach to city design should be brought into existence. This involves finding, first of all, some coherent administrative pattern to take the place of the present tangle of conflicting jurisdictions of territorial, county, and municipal authorities. It involves the incorporation of a more effective type of city planning authority in the very structure of the municipal government.

About the composition for such an authority, there appear to be many differences of opinion in Honolulu. Some favor a continuance of the purely advisory form of commission; some favor a more active and responsible type of commission. Few as yet, apparently, have questioned the usual commission form itself as the most desirable type of administrative organ. Most city planning authority in the United States is indeed vested in commissions. Often they are unpaid, as with the present Honolulu City Planning Commission. Sometimes they are paid, as in the new commission provided under the reformed charter of the City of New York. Such commissions tend to suffer from the lack of an indispensable element: a dominant personality of marked administrative or designing talent, capable of fusing together in a common design the special projects needed, anticipating future developments, making ready for them, installing them successfully, making them intelligible and useful to the community at large. Most of the effective planning in New York during the past five years has been due to the existence of such a personality as the head of the park system.* Wherever one

---

* This appreciation of much of Mr. Moses' early work I would not withdraw; but in view of his inability to tolerate, still less profit by, criticism I would now be inclined to throw safeguards around such a

encounters the highest type of planning work, one discovers such a personality, such a mind at the head of it. The vast and complicated regional planning reorganization of the Ruhr district in Germany was largely the work of a single man, Dr. Wilhelm Schmidt, who had charge of the regional development of the Ruhr until the advent of the Nazis. Similarly, in Hamburg the street development of the new areas along the Alster, the planning of the new parks, the building of the new schools, was largely the work of Dr. Fritz Schumacher.

Commissions are, by their very nature, consultative and deliberative bodies rather than executive ones. They provide a useful check upon the planner. They give no guarantee, in their own composition, of the ability to plan: rather the reverse. To establish the type of planning service needed, one person must be entrusted with the necessary power and responsibility. He must devote himself wholeheartedly to this single purpose: he must carry it in mind day and night; he must live with his plans; he must nurture them; he must guide their development; he must be capable of amending them. Such devotion and such integrated action are beyond the normal working of any commission, no matter how harmonious. For this reason, I propose that the active planning agents of the city be placed on a different footing, and I would put forward for discussion an organization on the following lines:

1. *A popular educational body, in this to be called the City Planning Council.* Such a council should be of an advisory nature. It should be non-paid. It should incorporate the major professional and occupational and religious groups

personality by giving the popular educational body, suggested later, a more positive political function, in a resolute effort to check the aberrations to which the will-to-power is always subject.

of the city—not excluding the responsible labor unions. This would bring into the active work of city planning groups like the medical professions, whose advice and interest have been regrettably lacking from this field—and whose failure to deal with the environment as a conditioning factor in disease has been a serious handicap, many observers think, to the profession itself.

The purpose of such a council, composed of the best available representatives of each group, should be twofold: a. to contribute their special professional advice toward the general development of the city, and b. to transmit to their special groups the concepts, the principles, and the vision of the more active city planning administration.

One danger in connection with appointments for such a body should be noted. In most cities, such appointments are treated as a way of paying off, by an honorary office, some minor political or personal debt; the purpose of advisory bodies that do not effectively advise is to serve as a front of respectability for the job in hand. It is not such a body that I have in mind; respectability and good intentions are not a sufficient qualification for the office. The council should not consist of more than fifteen members: these men should be distinguished primarily for their competence in their professional fields; they should still be active, and aggressively interested in their vocations, as well as in the general welfare of the city. They should not *pass* upon any specific measures; but they should help to form and criticize and assay the fundamental policies of the city planning administration. The members of such a body should be chosen at yearly intervals; in such a way as to give at least half of those first inducted a term of office as long as that of the Plan Director.

2. A Plan Director with a competent staff large enough to handle all the problems of survey, engineering, architec-

ture, and economics that may arise. The post of Plan Director should be an appointive one and it should hold for a relatively long period: probably for no less than ten years. A shorter span of office either does not permit the occupant to show his abilities, or it commits him, perhaps against his will, to a premature effort to achieve an effect.

It might be that in Honolulu, the type of man required for such a post could, like the Chairman of the Park Board, be obtained on a non-salaried basis. It is important, at all events, that he should be placed beyond the need for currying political favors, and that his work should be judged not by its immediate results in any particular year but by its total effect upon the city over the longer period of his supervision.

In giving the Plan Director the key position, I purposely would open the office to another type of expert guidance than that of the architect or the engineer. What is needed is someone who will understand the business of planning, organization, and co-ordination without necessarily being competent to carry through the actual task of design. This does not exclude the use of a person with an architectural or engineering training: it does exclude the use of his special services in the detailed work of carrying out the plan.

To obtain the best talent available for the latter work—and nothing less than the best should be good enough for Honolulu—the salary scale for permanent officials is too low. Hence all except the routine order of planning should be done with the part-time services of the best technician available. His selection should be mainly the responsibility of the Plan Director. Such an arrangement is not perhaps as satisfactory as would be the appointment of a city architect, who is both administrator and technician in one, on the traditional lines of certain European cities; but in the case of Honolulu, it offers the best method, I believe, of obtaining the superior technical equipment necessary for the work, along with that continuity in office and continued supervision which are indispensable to any long-term improvement.

3. *A collaborating Board of Public Works, consisting of the elected officials who administer the various city departments.* The active interest and understanding of these departments, together with such special members as the Park Board itself, are involved in every city planning program.

This Board of Works should meet regularly to discuss its common problems, and it should be brought together at special meetings on the initiative of the Plan Director when some new proposal, not covered by its routine procedure, is on the carpet.

Most people in Honolulu are by now agreed, I believe, that the present elective term of two years for city supervisors is far too short to permit effective public service. In New York, the term of the city officials was changed from two years to four years, with a marked advantage to competent officials and good administration. A term of at least four years, and probably not more than six, would be advisable in Honolulu if the right sort of administrator is to be drawn into public work.

It will occur to the student of municipal government that the post of Plan Director, as here outlined, corresponds on the planning and development side to that of Mayor or City Manager on the administrative side. This scheme would, it seems to me, combine the advantage of concentration of authority with the necessary democratic safeguards against abuse of power, and also with the necessary enlistment of interest and goodwill on the part of the municipal officials whose assent and resistance will in the long run make or mar most of the projects that the Plan Director may put forward. Before such an administrative board could be formed, however, it would be necessary, I believe, to group the existing city and county and territorial authorities into a more symmetrical board without the overlapping and conflicting jurisdictions that now exist.

The aim of this whole plan would be at once to widen the participation of citizens and professional groups in the entire program of city development, and to give more authority to technical competence and sound administrative initiative than now exists. Most city plan commissions, instead of grasping and interpreting general questions of policy, spend far too much time on niggling details, that often embarrass or block the designer of a project without contributing effectively to the formulation of general policy. A clear definition of the several functions involved in city planning (namely: planning itself, administration, and advisory counsel) is a first step toward sound collaboration. Plato's age-old dictum that the main concern in morals and government is for each agent to mind his own business, is still true. But this involves, first of all discovering what one's business truly is, and it involves the creation of a method of procedure whereby common business no less than individual business may be efficiently furthered. The advisory board would have no direct responsibility for determining policy but it would act as a liaison group between the public at large and the Plan Director and the Board of Works. As citizen-like interest in planning develops, however, and as the various organized bodies that make up the city become conscious of the scope of their own professional contribution to a city plan program, one may expect the advisory board to grow in importance.

14. THE FUNCTION OF THE PLAN DIRECTOR

Before discussing in more detail the functions of the Plan Director, let me anticipate some of the criticisms that may be laid against the provision of such an officer.

The first that naturally occurs is that the Director has an authority almost equal to that of the Mayor's: hence the possibility of rivalry and conflict and cross purposes. This objection need not detain us very long. Within the province of city planning, the Plan Director would indeed have a power comparable to the Mayor's; but like that of the Mayor himself, it would be subject to budgetary supervision and control. If the question be raised, why should not the city planning and administrative offices both be entrusted to an elected official like the Mayor, the answer is twofold:

a. The far-sighted planning of the structures of the city is by itself a full-time office. It calls for a different type of administrative ability from that of a mayor or city manager; and

b. The temperament that goes best with the professional capacities of the Plan Director is not necessarily that which allies itself easily with the tactful shoving and hauling and backing of ordinary political life.

The sort of city planner that may be needed is perhaps not to be drawn from the local community. He must therefore be brought here by appointment, and any effort to tie him to the routine of elected office would compromise his work from the very beginning. In a certain city on the West Coast, the municipal engineer, who for practical purposes is there the equivalent of the Plan Director, has devoted a great part of the time nominally supposed to be spent at the service of the city, in electioneering in local neighborhoods and in obtaining small municipal favors for these local groups. As a result of such canny efforts, he has achieved wide popularity and a very powerful political backing, although his actual contribution to the planning of the city as a whole is very largely a negative one. The second objection that may be raised to the office of Plan Director is that it provides for too great a concentration of power. But power as such is not necessarily an evil. What must be guarded against is irresponsible power, power that is above criticism, power that is above the possibility of being displaced or overthrown. Plainly, a Plan Director, although he would be given a final say over many important points in a city's development—some of which would lay him open to the temptations of bribery and graft, or even merely affable collusion—would be subject to the normal checks of democracy: public criticism, arraignment on charges, and dismissal in the event of proved incompetence or crime.

What our American cities have suffered from is the lack of power on the part of those duly commissioned to further the city's activities. Our cities have suffered—thanks to backward Constitutional interpretations by the Supreme Courts—from the inability to acquire land in advance of public need, to control the socially negligent practices of the individual property owner or land speculator, and in many States to make positive provision for the housing of lower-income groups not taken care of under decent standards by the commercial builder. To create the office of a Plan Director or of a city plan commission without considerably widening the powers of the existing municipal governments eventually, through local and constitutional amendments, is to give with one hand and take back with the other: to promise the results of planning without providing the elementary means of achieving those results.

The greatest safeguard against the misuse of power is the

active employment of scientific knowledge and technical skill. The physician has the power of life and death over his patient—a power that the community willingly entrusts to those who have sufficiently prepared themselves by study and discipline to wield it. So, too, with the Plan Director, the safeguard against despotism or caprice is the same as the safeguard against ignorance and incompetence: namely, in the very technique that the engineer and the architect and the planner have achieved for arriving at their results.*

The basic guide to all comprehensive city planning is the survey of the city. This should be a body of knowledge in the process of continual development and revision, which will show, both at large and in detail, the essential characteristics of the city and its region with respect to the geological formation, the soil, topography, climate, weather, water and other natural resources, occupations and industries, and the social and educational and religious practices of the community. These surveys must be prepared with the aid of competent specialists and technicians in each department, and they should be paralleled by similar activities in the schools of the city.

All such surveys begin with actual outdoor observation. This intimate knowledge of the city, deepening with years and experience, should be the possession of every citizen. City planning bodies that lack such understanding themselves, and that fail to foster such understanding on the part of the individuals and groups who compose the city, lack the very first resource of intelligent planning: a basis in fact, a

---

* This assertion I now regard as naïve. There is no despotism so hard to challenge as professional routine; and the more exacting and esoteric professional competence becomes the more carefully it needs to be watched. The insulation of the "expert" from lay criticism is too great a temptation to which to subject even the most able and conscientious.

true picture of existing conditions, a many-sided contact with the life and activities whose physical structure they purpose to improve. While in most cities, city museums serve merely an antiquarian interest, it should be possible in Honolulu to create a civic museum, as part of a wider city planning project, which would deal with the future as well as the past and which would be the natural repository of the knowledge acquired in the Plan Director's office. In such museums, the past, the present, and the future of Honolulu should be spread before the eye in such a concentrated and simplified fashion that every citizen might become an intelligent and active participant in the city's destiny.*

Following the survey, the next important task of the Plan Director is the development of a comprehensive policy for urban renewal: that is, for maintaining and conserving all that is sound in Honolulu's actual development up to the present, and for introducing such major changes and innovations as are necessary for the maintenance of health and well-being in future. The formulation of such a program and its critical revision is something which may bring to the surface divergent and sometimes incompatible interests. So far from shunning such issues, as officialdom everywhere too often timorously is tempted to, the Plan Director must, for the sake of the work that is to be carried through, dare to dramatize them and bring them to a head. For the notion that any important changes can be made in the structure of our present cities without also changing the general pattern of life which they exemplify and reflect, is a superstition. Planning, so far from attempting merely to stabilize existing practices, rather concerns itself with achieving an orderly basis for change and readjustment. In working toward this

---

* I would underline this proposal, and draw it to the attention of both educator and planner.

end, it will necessarily come into conflict with vested economic interests of one kind or another. In the long run, good planning works to the advantage of all the inhabitants of a city: not the least to the advantage of those who have a large economic stake in its existence. But by this very token, it cannot forfeit the advantage of the whole to the temporary aggrandizement or interest of any single individual or group.

This should come out very plainly in Honolulu, if any effective city planning is to be done, in the steps that must be taken to deal with the present land situation. It will come out likewise in various other departments. Such changes as may be projected can come about only through a well-considered program of education and purposive political action. They cannot be bought on the cheap. One of the important reasons for putting the Plan Director above the petty concerns of local politics, and above fear of losing office through temporary shifts and eddies in public sentiment, lies in the very need for the exertion on his part of courageous leadership.

The third step in arriving at an effective scheme of city development is the provision of a master plan which will not merely record the existing development of the city but which will indicate the lines of future development, both in space and in time. Such a plan is not to be regarded as a monument, forever fixed and inflexible. It is rather to be looked upon as an instrument of orderly thought, open to revision as need dictates from year to year and from generation to generation. *But in the preparation of such a plan, I must emphasize the importance of the time element. A good city plan not merely rests upon an historic sense of the city's development in the past, but it assigns to each new project its desirable order in time.* Premature developments are expensive developments. Retarded developments, such as the belated provision of schools or playgrounds after land has risen to a value which makes its acquisition all but impossible, are expensive developments. To achieve economy in city design means not merely to invest the municipality's capital in the right sort of structure, but to provide for its building at the right time. Not merely must there be a systematic study of the timely arrangement of urban projects, but there must be a priority schedule in terms of social value. Without such a priority schedule, public monies are forever in danger of being quickly expended upon the simpler and more obvious forms of urban reconstruction, while more important ones, because of their difficulty or because of the total cost involved, are indefinitely postponed while evils pile up and grievances become more deep-seated.*

Finally, it should be the province of the Plan Director not merely to formulate, with the assistance of the Board of Works, a policy and a program of planning: he should also have the power to initiate necessary improvements and, where no existing authority is competent to undertake them, to supervise their construction. In the case of public projects involving the collaboration of one or more city departments, the major responsibility for co-ordination and control should rest with the Plan Director.

The broad powers I have outlined seem to me essential to the economic development of the city of the future. They

---

* In his diatribe against planning in The Good Society, Mr. Walter Lippmann has said that a plan that can be changed is not a plan. If that were true his case against planning of any kind would be justified. But what he says applies only to bad planning. Good planning does not attempt to fix structures but to guide processes. The ability to meet fresh emergents—and fresh emergencies—is precisely what makes planning more effective than stolid routine or unco-ordinated change. The static conception of plan is as inapplicable to a city's development as to a military campaign, though in the former the rate of change is far slower.

are democracy's responsible alternative to the irrational and irresponsible processes of dictatorship. They are also democracy's alternative to the log-rolling, the wire-pulling, the ineffectual jockeying, and the massive inert mediocrity of American municipal politics, as practiced in most cities up to this last generation. The important changes which must be instituted cannot be achieved more cheaply. We cahnot remain in our old groove without sinking deeper. It requires an act of political imagination and courage to achieve anything like the organization that is needed today to cope with the problems that the disorderly and incompetent development of the American city have raised.

Whether Honolulu has the type of leadership necessary to create such an office, and to give it understanding and support, I do not know. Possibly as yet no one knows. But this one may safely say: if the right lead is given and if the responsibility is accepted, there is perhaps no place better situated than Honolulu to achieve favorable results.

15. CONCLUSION AND SUMMARY

Although broad views and principles should have emerged from the foregoing description of Honolulu's needs and opportunities, let me attempt to sum them up:

The first of these is that we are approaching the era of stabilization and that the time for long-range planning and for systematic co-ordinated planning is already upon us. We are now about to create the durable framework of the city. Whatever is done toward urban improvement should be done well. It should be done not by mere rote and habit, as cheaply as possible, as conventionally as possible. It should be done rather out of the fullest inquiry into the best contemporary city planning methods, and out of the fullest determination to achieve the sort of political organization that is necessary to put such projects through. Honolulu's parks, for example, are already, despite the short term of their development, well abreast of the past generation's best work, in many departments. They have now, like the city itself, to be more fully adapted to the new needs and the new plans that are characteristic of twentieth century practice.

The second basic principle is that park planning is a coordinate branch of city planning. There can be no effective park planning on a grand scale without working out a unified attack upon Honolulu's city planning problems as a whole: renewal of its blighted districts, the replacement of its slums, the opening up of its middle-class suburban subdivisions, and the restriction of a premature and uneconomic suburban development.

The third principle is that a comprehensive park system, like a comprehensive plan for the city as a whole, must be worked out in systematic fashion. It must be based upon a deliberate survey of resources, needs, and opportunities. It must provide for development in both space and time. And it must be established in accordance with a social scale of values which will put the major social needs of the population first and be entirely free from any tendency to respond erratically to local pressures and sporadic individual suggestions.

The fourth principle I would emphasize is one that applies particularly to the Park Board: In the development of the city, the park program remains the very core of a more social conception of city development. The Park Board itself, therefore, has a very urgent responsibility to assume the leadership here, to introduce to the community as a whole the more comprehensive designs for parks, parkways, and neighborhood developments. It has the duty of taking the initiative in furthering popular education as to what plan and design may mean in life: first, by bringing all of its present structures up to the high standard of excellence that two or three of them have already achieved; and second, by interpreting the nature of such plan and design to the community at large. Here is a field of effort that should enlist the best talents of this generation. Here is something that should call into quickened activity the hopes and resources and dreams of the young, the experience and fortitude of the old. Out of the shabbiness and messiness of the present city, a new order may emerge; and out of its natural charm, a maturer beauty—more deeply humanized, more friendly to human desire—may be constructed. Only two things are needed: not the power of execution, but the imagination to conceive and the courage to desire.

THE SOCIAL FOUNDATIONS
OF POST-WAR BUILDING

EDITORIAL FOREWORD, BY F. J. OSBORN

Mr. Lewis Mumford has written the following essay in response to a request for a contribution to our thought about town and country planning problems on this side of the Atlantic. It is another form of American aid to Britain, on generous lease-lend terms. Those who have read The Culture of Cities will not need to be reminded that Mr. Mumford's study of the urban problem covers a wider range of interests, and delves more deeply into fundamentals, than that of any other writer, and that it transcends national boundaries and local variations. His analysis discloses and evaluates facts and trends that are common to cities in America and Britain, if not in all parts of the world. At the same time he is well aware that every country, and indeed every city, exhibits its own special variants of the common problem. Therefore in sending me what he calls "a telescopic long-distance view" of our planning situation, he expressed some fear that in writing a pamphlet designed to have meaning in two countries he may have included some references unintelligible to British readers, and he authorized me to make such alterations as I considered necessary. But in fact I have not had to change more than three words.

This essay carries a stage further the line of thought de-

veloped in The Culture of Cities and Faith for Living. The former book, I think, already takes rank as a classic of urban sociology, integrating for the first time the physical elements in town structure with the familial, social, economic, political, moral, and esthetic elements, and succeeding to a remarkable degree in placing all these in long-term historical perspective. The latter is a tract for our times, comminatory and disturbing, yet productive of lasting inspiration to those who have the will to make the best that can be made of this difficult world. Both books have been widely read in this country. But I doubt if the radical character of their criticism of our present urban civilization has been equally widely grasped. Mr. Mumford is a revolutionary thinker, not in the sense of one who plots the curve of existing organizational trends and logically extrapolates that curve to infinity (he would dismiss that sort of exercise as mere "automatic thinking"), but in the sense of one who burrows down to neglected fundamentals—the plainest human biological needs, the most obvious aspirations of ordinary men and women—and works out what modern science, skill, and creative energy could do to satisfy these if to satisfy them were the conscious aim of society. He is no more a disciple of Rousseau than of Marx. He neither revolts against mechanical progress nor accepts its current or developing forms as inevitable. But he does revolt against the "devitalized mechanisms, desocialized organisms, and depersonalized societies" which the uncritical acceptance of industrialism and urbanism have produced.

In rating Mr. Mumford's contribution to the sum of thought on the problems of civilization as of first-class importance, it is not necessary to agree with him in every detail. One may doubt, for example, whether he is right in his view that Man has exhausted the possibilities of his dream of mechanical power, or is yet disposed to think he has. That is a

*question of dates. But I am sure Mr. Mumford is right in his
main thesis—that we have to a dangerous extent lost sight of
the objects of all our mechanism and organization, and that
the task of the next age is "a fresh canvass of human ideals
and human purposes," a re-assessment of the scale of values
by which social progress shall be judged. In the field of city
reconstruction, owing to the war-time pause, we have a particular opportunity of a new start. What Mr. Mumford has to
say on this aspect of our post-war problems is therefore of
very present and urgent interest. He places high in his list of
aims: space for living; cultural as well as physical decentralization to country towns; the bringing together of urban and
rural pursuits and interests; and the revivification of regional
economies and societies. Though the texture of Mr. Mumford's presentation is very different from that of a Royal
Commission, it is significant that in principle his conclusions
are those of the Barlow Report. And the great objectives to
which he gives priority are practicable objectives for Britain
with the instruments we now have, or can have, in our hands.*

*Welwyn Garden City,
December 1942.*

[This paper was first printed in the Re-Building Britain Series, No. 9.
It is here reprinted with the kind permission of Faber and Faber, Ltd.]

---

1. THE ULTIMATE ISSUES

In our anticipations of post-war planning, perhaps the most
important thing to remember is that our task is not the simple
one of rebuilding demolished houses and ruined cities. If
only the material shell of our society needed repair, our de-

signs might follow familiar patterns. But the fact is our task
is a far heavier one; it is that of replacing an outworn civilization. The question is not how much of the superstructure
should be replaced, but how much of the foundations can be
used for a new set of purposes and for a radically different
mode of life.

There is a sense in which the demolition that is taking
place through the war has not yet gone far enough. Though
many of the past structures are still serviceable, and some
of them truly venerable, the bulk of our building no longer
corresponds to the needs and possibilities of human life. We
must therefore continue to do, in a more deliberate and rational fashion, what the bombs have done by brutal hit-or-
miss, if we are to have space enough to live in and produce
the proper means of living.

In short, the crisis we are now in the midst of does not
admit of a return to our original condition, in the fashion
that a crisis in pneumonia, once surmounted, enables the
patient to recover his original health. The fact is that, before
the war, there was spiritually little health in us. Our elaborate mechanical organization of life had resulted in an increasingly purposeless society, in which the parts were neatly
articulated and ordered, while the whole made little sense
to the common man in terms of life-satisfactions and life-
fulfillments. A great part of our material shell was confused,
inefficient, depressing: but what was even worse was the
growing realization that, at its most efficient best, it was
empty.

There were a few people, like Albert Schweitzer, who perceived this fact at the end of the last world war: but at that
time the word "reconstruction" was still uppermost in people's minds; for it still seemed that the society Western man
had created before 1914 was essentially durable, and de-

served to be continued. Today words like rebuilding and reconstruction betray a failure to recognize the extent and depth of the change that lies before us. For the fact is that the drama and plot that held men's minds for the last four or five hundred years have now reached the catastrophic fifth act; and the scenery and stage-equipment for this drama will soon be as useless for the new story as the typical characters who are now, with a final flourish of trumpets, making their exits.

Western man has exhausted the possibilities of the dream of mechanical power, which has so long dominated his imagination; he is now the self-betrayed victim of those who would utilize that power for the fulfillment of debased and irrational purposes, barbarizing man instead of subduing and humanizing nature. We live in a world given over to devitalized mechanisms, desocialized organisms, and depersonalized societies: a world that has lost its sense of the ultimate dignity of the person as completely as the Roman Empire did, at the height of its military greatness and technical facility. The farther we follow this road, the more hopelessly we shall be lost.

The signs of this exhaustion are many; one of the most critical of them is an unwillingness to play the game if the player happens to be losing. When people are really interested in a life-theme, they cling to it even under the most adverse conditions; indeed, the pressure of difficulty only intensifies their interest. When the Christian theme was in the making, persecutions welded the faithful together and finally resulted in a unified church which could exercise power; when the interests of capitalism were coalescing, adventurous enterprisers accepted losses and bankruptcies without wincing, and began all over again: the Christian did not cease to believe in his religion because it brought personal grief,

or the capitalist in capitalism because it might result in personal ruin.

But we have seen just the opposite of this in our time.
Capitalists accepted the closing down of the world-market
just as democratic peoples accepted, without a counter-move-
ment, the advance of a cancerous totalitarianism. Why? Because a counter-effort implied risk and sacrifice; and risk
and sacrifice were not accepted, since the faith that would
have made them self-justifying had evaporated. Had the plot
become too complicated to follow? Had the drama itself
become meaningless through repetition? I shall attempt presently to answer that question. But the fact to be noted is that
the old game no longer thrills the players. If Americans had
really loved their motor cars, as much as the Manchester
manufacturers of the early nineteenth century loved their
cotton mills, the American fleet would have carried the war
to Japan before the occupation of Indo-China.

In general, one may say that in the present crisis nothing
was real enough to fight for, in the more civilized countries,
because nothing was significant enough to live for. It was
only the countries that had recast the old drama, the drama
of racial superiority and world conquest, that had the energy
to seize the initiative on behalf of their destructive purposes.
This is a matter that bears heavily on every plan for improvement. When the Roman Empire was collapsing, it was
useless to plan for the extension of aqueducts or postal services; what constructive energy was available went properly
into churches and monasteries. So we must scrutinize every
proposal for future building to be sure that we are not the
victims of automatic thinking; the most elaborate setting for
the old drama may be so much empty stage lumber in terms
of the life we mean to live. The first step in adequate planning today is to make a fresh canvass of human ideals and

human purposes. All that was good in our past way of life will stand up under that scrutiny; all that was cheap, superficial, morbid, or emptily materialistic will fall away.

If the old plot has become meaningless, the scenery against which the action has taken place is even more irrelevant. The great capital cities of the last four hundred years, in which military might and social luxury were massed, can no longer be the ultimate expression of human desire. In the universal products of our mechanical civilization, like the radio, the telephone, and the cinema, they share their proudest achievements with the meanest village; their very size, moreover, has reduced the opportunity of their inhabitants to participate in the parade of fashion and taste. As for the great industrial towns of the last two centuries, in which people swarmed together in grimy regimented streets, to take part in the daily battle of production—these cities were the stage of ambitions that have ceased to be real and of achievements that have become increasingly hollow. No money income could make amends for a life-confinement in these dreary infernos: counter-irritants, narcotics, aphrodisiacs, mechanized fantasies only increase the debasement they seem to alleviate.

Once, perhaps, the blight and misery of these cities could be speciously justified: they were symbols of enterprise; they were monuments to mechanical ingenuity in which the age rejoiced; they were, at the lowest, a source of vast profits to ground landlords, speculative builders, industrial enterprisers, and small groups or classes gained, even if the general good was ruthlessly sacrificed and the entire environment befouled. More hopefully, under the doctrine of progress, they were steps to a better society.

But even these narrow private gains are no longer in prospect. Private enterprise, still hoping for past gains, pre-

vents the centers of our cities from being adequately rebuilt;
and as a result, those who wish better conditions find a temporary surcease, if not an effective permanent solution, on
the outskirts. Where the automobile has been most freely
used, the disorganization and disruption of our urban centers
is most marked; Los Angeles and Detroit, both largely the
creations of this new machine, are also its most conspicuous
victims. But in one degree or another, the tendency to plan-
less dispersion is world-wide; in a hundred futile ways people seek an individual solution for their social problem, and
so ultimately create a second social problem.

The prewar migration to suburban cottages, to week-end
huts, to rural estates, was a recognition of the fact that our
typical urban environments no longer offer the possibility
of a significant or healthy life. Something more genial to the
human soul is desired: contact with the soil, the discipline
of manual labor, more intimate companionship with one's
fellows, the esthetic joys of sunrise and sunset, of passing
cloud and rising moon; and in the search for these fundamental qualities many people temporarily forget that social
intercourse and social co-operation are no less important.
Biologically, the rural scene is more adequate; but the inva-
sions and perversions of a dying civilization contaminate
even the countryside; roadside slums are reminders of the
social insufficiency of mere escapism.

In America, where in some respects the mischiefs of contemporary urban civilization have been carried farthest, the
greater part of our overgrown metropolises are, in strict economic terms, bankrupt: their dwindling taxes cannot support
the load of debt incurred through growth, disorganization,
and blight; and their urgent repair awaits a systematic de-
flation of the still absurd structure of values that was created
in the past, in anticipation of further growth. The "increase

of population and wealth" has become a purely ironic term; depopulation and bankruptcy are indicated.*

Temporarily, the need to conserve existing utilities, the inability to fabricate new quarters, the necessity to dispense with private motor transportation because of the shortage of rubber or petrol may reverse some of the surface tendencies. But the underlying facts will remain; and the chief of these is the vast secular change that crept upon us almost unawares: the end of the Era of Expansion and of all the premises upon which it was based.

2. THE END OF EXPANSION

The world crisis that has now lasted for the lifetime of an entire generation indicates that a radical shift in the direction of social movement has taken place: an age of expansion is giving way to an age of stabilization. So far this change has been a blind and blundering one, because the underlying causes have been neglected, and because, furthermore, the interests and attitudes that were formed by a tradition of expansion prevented us from interpreting the facts that lay open before us. Quite superficial events—trade rivalries between nations, the murder of a Grand Duke, the treaty of Versailles, the resurgence of tyranny in government—have been treated as sufficient explanations for the more profound forces that have been at work.

This is not to say that the pressure of the present crisis would not have been altered by intelligent intervention. Without a deliberate exploitation of the forces of evil, by men whose contempt for the human is truly pathological, the crisis would not so soon have reached the catastrophic dimensions of the present disorder nor produced such unbearable

---

* The war boom, with its congested housing and its superficial prosperity, marks a temporary reprieve, not a permanent transformation.

agonies. In that case, what is now happening swiftly under the pressure of the Nazi assault, would have come about slowly, and perhaps in the long run, more fatally, for a disease that too long escapes diagnosis may progress so far that the patient is past cure. But the flight from reality which characterized democratic statesmanship was itself a grievous symptom of decay. In any event, the crisis was inevitable; for, in the drama of expansion, Western man had reached the last act.

The present is a painful interregnum between two eras. The first began roughly in the fifteenth century; it is associated with the rise of capitalism, militarism, and mechanization; and it had as its object the expansion of man's power over Nature and of Western man's power, in particular, over the more amiable or more feebly armed peoples who inhabited the rest of the planet. The outlines of the period that approaches are not so easy to characterize; for most of the characters have still to be invented and the lines have yet to be written; but one may call it, by way of broad contrast, a period of stabilization. Some of the painful struggles and perversions of the present age are due to the fact that we are still trying to apply the method appropriate to a period of expansion to a social organization that must be devoted to the contrary task of stabilization. In this spirit, Americans during the depression of the thirties were still dreaming of a new mechanical gadget, or a new industry, which would renew the cycle of industrial expansion and commercial profit. Today, while a rational economy will welcome substantial technological improvements, like radar or magnesium alloys, it cannot treat them as a means of salvation.

The facts about the past and the approaching era are familiar to students of history and sociology; but the interpretation of these facts has been tardy. Strangely enough,

our present dilemma was accurately foreseen by John Stuart
Mill, in what has become, by force of events, a great chapter
in the second volume of his Principles of Political Economy.
That chapter is devoted to a discussion of what Mill somewhat misleadingly calls the "Stationary State": one in which
the area of new capital investments has dwindled, in which
through birth control, the population tends to become stationary, and in which the rates of profit and interest tend to
fall toward zero.

That is the chapter which everyone knows by only a single
sentence, one in which Mill doubted whether labor-saving
machinery had yet lightened the day's burden of a single
worker; but it was here that he made a far more significant
observation: namely, that a state of dynamic equilibrium,
though it might be dreaded by the profiteer, was the condition required for translating mechanical improvements into
social welfare. In re-stating Mill's observation as history, I
only accentuate the merit of his own contribution as prophecy.

The era of Western expansion had three overlapping and
interacting phases: land expansion; population expansion;
industrial expansion. The break-up of the medieval ideology
in the fourteenth and fifteenth centuries released men for the
performance of a fresh drama; gunpowder, the compass, and
the three-masted sailing ship made their conquest of the
lands beyond Europe possible, and the zeal of the new mer-
chants systematized the agents of exploitation. The new machine technology substituted an automaton for a person as
the embodiment of reason and order in society; instead of
seeking for the just man made perfect, men sought for perfection in the power machine, made progressively more automatic.

Though many other channels of life remained, the dominant flow of interest, intelligence, and desire was canalized

by the machine; and though Western man carried with him into other parts of the world his arts and sciences, not least his theology, his claim to dominance over others was the result of the weapons and machines that multiplied his power. In our own lifetime this whole process has come to an end, or very rapidly approaches an end. Other peoples, who a hundred years ago existed on a primitive level, have fast become masters of the Western instrumentalities and producers in their own right. And at the very moment that Western man loses his claims to monopoly, he has also become self-critical and distrustful of the life to which he once so wholeheartedly committed himself. He demands a special price for further mechanization: bread and shows. He must be bribed and coaxed to perform acts that his forefathers performed gladly, wholeheartedly, with conviction. Bread and shows mean conquest, brutality, and psychic disintegration: symptoms that have been painfully evident even in countries that have seemingly escaped the poisons of nazism. But before modern man will invent a new drama, he must perhaps be convinced that the old one is, in fact, ended. Here, then, are the proofs and indications.

3. THE CLOSE OF THE WORLD FRONTIER

Land expansion was the prime source of the industrialization that took place, at a rising tempo, after the seventeenth century. This process had both a material and a psychological result. By opening up hitherto unexplored tracts of the earth, Western man had added to the world's area of arable land; he drew on rich food resources, like maize and cocoa and the potato, no less than on the Newfoundland fisheries; and he added to his technical armory by utilizing Indian cotton, Chinese porcelain, and Amazonian rubber. Psychologically, the effect of the expansion was exhilarating; it gave him a literally boundless confidence in his own inventions, his own theological beliefs, his own aptitude to rule over other peoples. This expansion of the individual ego, which made possible the feats of the conquistadors like Cortez or Pizarro, took on a collective coloring by the nineteenth century, and it pushed over into other departments of life. Cities expanded their urban areas as if they, too, were illimitable.

By 1890, as an American historian, Frederick Jackson Turner, pointed out, the United States had reached the limits of its last frontier; the entire continental area had been staked out if not occupied; and the habits that were appropriate to a pioneer period were no longer in harmony with the new facts of existence. As a country, we could no longer evade the necessity for settling down and making the most of our resources; it was impossible to overcome the errors of gutting out the forests, mining the soils, or annihilating the wild life merely by moving on to a virgin area.

What is true of the settlement of the United States has, within the last generation, become true of the world at large: nothing remains for the explorer except barren mountain tops or polar wastes; what new areas remain for settlement are negligible; regions of difficulty like Manchuria, Siberia, or Alaska are the last important frontiers. The cycle of exploration and conquest and random appropriation is over; our problem is not to add to the existing land areas but to make better use of them, by systematically applying our new-found geological, climatic, biological, and social knowledge to the better ordering of man's estate; and by utilizing art and political imagination to create permanent quarters which will be favorable to a new set of purposes and a new myth. The period of land expansion has come to an end, and the hopes derived from it are no longer capable of sustaining our fresh efforts.

Do not deduce from this condition that the possibilities of new population movements are over; on the contrary, there are areas that are now sparsely occupied, like the Tennessee Valley and the Columbia River Valley, that will benefit by an added population; there are other areas, like the blighted areas of some of our great metropolises, which are due to be turned into park land, or even in some instances into market gardens, even as the rundown farms of the Adirondacks have been turned back into forest. Arid regions, from California to Australia, waiting to be harnessed to the sun, will become the Egypts of a new cycle of civilization. But this new population movement, this new re-settlement, cannot proceed from the same motives that governed the past; co-operation must replace conquest, and systematic cultivation must take the place of heedless and often destructive utilization.

The closing of the world frontier has been accompanied by the closing down of national frontiers; barriers to human travel and immigration were raised, two decades before the open war of 1939, that would have seemed incredible in the nineteenth century; the irrational response of isolationism and autarchy has aggravated the condition itself, increased the economic and political frustrations, and provided the conditions for deadly strife between regional and national cultures whose very existence has been based upon the maintenance of the world market. That way lies chaos: chaos and savagery.

While the process of land expansion postponed the period of regional stabilization until the limits of expansion had been reached, the fact that these limits have now been reached must be accepted as a basic condition. Utopia can no longer be an unknown land on the other side of the globe;

it is, rather, the land one knows best, reapportioned, reshaped, and recultivated for permanent human occupation. This conclusion makes imperative in our age what was still only an ideal possibility at the time when Ebenezer Howard outlined his project for the first Garden City: the internal recolonization of every country.

4. THE STABILIZATION OF INDUSTRY

The discovery and exploitation of the relatively open lands outside Europe was followed by an expansion of mechanized industry. Mechanization was a far more widespread process than people usually understand; it touched the intellectual life through printing, the military sphere through the reintroduction of systematic drill, and agricultural practice through the new process of drilling or planting seed in orderly rows, no less than it touched the fabrication of standardized articles by specialized labor and specialized machines.

The success of the machine was due to the cheapened cost of production, partly through more systematic effort, partly through the use of non-human agents of power, like water, wind, steam, and electricity. But two other facts made the expansion of the machine economy both possible and profitable.

One of these was the application of the machine to realms of life where it had heretofore never been utilized, even in primitive form: the railroad and the electric light are examples. The economists' doctrine of increasing wants was a generalization of this possibility of performing mechanically actions that men had never done before, except in fantasy, like communicating at a distance. The other condition for the profitable spread of the machine was the existence of a disparity in the standard of living between the workers engaged in producing the raw materials on colonial territories or the finished products in the factories, and the classes that bought these products.

Plainly it was the unevenness in purchasing power between the Western nations and the more primitive civilizations they exploited that accounted for a large share of the profits. Within each country, the existence of an "internal proletariat," as Toynbee has aptly called it, performed the same function. The whole tempo of industrial expansion would have been many beats slower from the beginning if the industrial workers had been adequately fed, clothed, housed, and educated. Machines produced profits and the profits were partly plowed in, as capital, to produce new machines, wherever a fresh opportunity offered, because the success of production was not gauged in terms of an adequate civic and domestic life for the population as a whole.

Now, during the pre-war years, three important changes have taken place in industry. One was the slowing down of the need for fresh capital goods in that large part of the industrial system that has already been mechanized. Instead of the complete renovation of industry that took place during the nineteenth century, the opportunities for further mechanization occur only in new industries, like motor cars or wireless sets, or in industries directly serving war-production. Once a railway system is built, the further demand for steel rails and locomotives is on a replacement basis. The accomplished success of the machine, in other words, retards its further expansion; the wholesale nineteenth-century change from handicraft to machines, from hand power or wind power to steam or electricity can now take place only in the backward countries.

The second important change is the development of a state of chronic unemployment in the advanced industrial countries. While classic capitalism, throughout the nineteenth

century, maintained a pool of unemployed, which was useful
in meeting seasonal shifts and keeping down the wages of
labor, the enlargement of this pool calls attention to the fact
that the increased efficiency of the machine diminishes the
demand for labor, so long as there is no attempt to reappor-
tion the annual income and to direct production into socially
more useful channels. The unemployment of labor has been
accompanied by an equally significant unemployment of
capital: in both cases, it would seem, because the prospects
of profit no longer exist on the terms on which they were
offered in the past. Neither capital nor labor will accept the
conditions which fostered expansion in the past: the first
demands profits without risks; the second demands a living
wage without insecurity.

Both these demands involve a radical change in the existing institutional structure, which was adapted to an expanding economy. If capital will not take risks, it must not expect
high returns; it must consent to employment on the bare reward of keeping alive the productive system itself, and the
enterprisers who once so wholeheartedly devoted their lives
to industry for the sake of power and money alone, must now
look for more social incentives; * no matter how private
their enterprise, they must seek a larger satisfaction through
their function as quasi-public servants. Their market now depends upon a steady rise in popular purchasing power. This
means, in turn, a shift in capital investments from industries
promising a high profit to industries promising a better fulfillment of social need. Both the worker and the investor ask
for the same ultimate reward: security. And security is possible only in a stable economy.

The signs of this change are already numerous; the growth

* Even such a successful exponent of "free enterprise" as Lord Wool-
ton has now publicly accepted this fact.

of insurance during the last fifty years, the growth of industrial monopolies, the steady intervention of the State as a
participator in and a director of industrial enterprises all
indicate the widespread nature of the process. But up to the
present the stabilization that has taken place has been framed
largely in financial terms; standard wage rates, unemployment and old age insurance, old age pensions, tariffs and
subsidies—all these are attempts to secure stability by the
use of financial devices. Yet this financial stabilization is
itself as insecure as anything else in the world, since war
and monetary inflation can either separately or together
make a mockery of the entire structure. The conditions for
genuine industrial stabilization are, I shall presently suggest,
of an entirely different nature.

In fact, for the present, financial stabilization works
against the many-sided economic stabilization that must take
place. Take the case of the investment by insurance companies in urban real estate in the United States. These investments were calculated to produce a regular income so
long as the old conditions of expansion held; but during the
last ten years they have acted to prevent the necessary defla-
tion of values in metropolitan areas, which are essential to
their rebuilding; and because of this failure, the rebuilding
of urban areas, which is essential to a sounder economy, has
been delayed or, where it has taken place, has been miscon-
ceived and frustrated, repeating, as in the congested planning
of the Parkchester project in New York, the very blunders
a stable economy should avoid.

From the standpoint taken here, the stabilization of industry is inevitable; the conditions which favored expansion
during the last three centuries are definitely over; expansion
on the past terms is possible only for the purpose of waging
war. If stabilization should continue in purely pecuniary

terms, of monopoly, insurance, class privileges, the result will be self-defeating; whereas if it is resisted, it must lead to a complete breakdown of our whole economy, as took place throughout the world during the last decade; and this in turn can only lead to resuming the archaic pattern of conquest, pillage, inhuman exploitation, and even outright slavery, which the Germans have restored.

Before discussing the conditions of a balanced economy, as the essential foundation for the next step in human development, I wish to examine the third element that has significantly changed within our own time: the population. Here, too, a change of the first importance has taken place.

5. POPULATION EQUILIBRIUM

The third condition for the world-wide expansion that took place during the last five centuries, particularly during the last two, was the increase in population. This required for its existence an enormous increase in the food supply; and it was furthered during the nineteenth century by an improvement in diet, in hygienic regimen, and in the care of children.

During the nineteenth century, the greatest achievement in mass-production was the mass-production of human beings. Every new child was a consumer; and the basis for an expanding economy lay in this seemingly illimitable demand. On the prospect of continued population-increase, cities expanded, urban land values rose, and each further expansion was solidified in the financial structure itself. While this pressure continued, a temporary miscalculation which caused an overproduction or overcapitalization would eventually be rectified by population increase.

Around 1870 in England, somewhat earlier in France, and at various later dates in most other countries, this rising curve of population increase began to flatten out. Today most of the advanced industrial countries, with the exception of Holland, show a strong tendency toward equilibrium. Only peasant economies and countries, like Russia, still under pioneer conditions, show any considerable lag in reaching stabilization.

There are two sides to this tendency: one socially desirable, the other dubious. On one hand, it is an example of the general tendency to pass from quantitative to qualitative achievement: a mark of a higher civilization. Intelligent people wisely prefer three children, healthfully nurtured, carefully educated, to a dozen children brought up with insufficient food and other resources. To this extent, contraception indicates a rising standard of intelligence and civic responsibility. Aimless and uncontrolled breeding belongs to the lower orders of organic life, not to man.

But there is another side to the curbing of population growth which comes out as soon as one relates the survival statistics with the distribution of population according to the size and the nature of the habitat. This is the evident fact that fecundity is associated with a rural life and rural traditions, while sterility is associated with metropolitanism. In America, cities above 25,000 do not reproduce their population, and as the size of the city increases, the rate of population increase declines. Part of the curb, therefore, is due to the creation of an urban standard of expenditures and an urban routine that is hostile to reproduction; drab, crowded residential quarters in which children are unwelcome because the parents cannot afford an extra room; cities in which a sterile ideal of comfortable gentility has replaced the desire for the joys and anxieties of parental responsibility; social groups in which a rising level of fashionable expenditure leaves no surplus for the birth and care of children who, if they occur at all, do so in numbers insufficient to reproduce the stock. In short, urbanism results in a decline of animal faith; and without this faith there is no urge to reproduction. Without migration from the rural areas, the bigger towns would be steadily depopulated through their ineptitude for life.

When these facts are treated statistically, in the gross, they seem to point to a gradual tapering away of life in the more civilized countries of the world: at best to a mere holding of their own. But these changes have all taken place as a result of human choices, human inventions, human scientific advances; and they can be modified, or the tendencies indicated reversed, by other inventions, other choices. If stabilization be accepted as a temporary goal, which will allow a breathing space after a period of unlimited expansion, a shift in the incidence of births would seem as desirable as a geographic resettlement of the population.

The overbreeding of the peasants and the proletariat, until their social and economic opportunities are improved, is as undesirable as the underbreeding of the rest of the population; the remedy for the first is better conditions for living, that for the second, a less ignoble scheme of maintaining status and security. Without succumbing to premature and probably prejudiced conclusions about the biological value of one part or another of the population, the social remedy in both cases points to a similar goal.

In a catastrophic period like the present one, it would be a grave sin for the peoples of the more advanced countries to permit their love of physical ease to make them lose sight of their biological responsibilities. For all its defects, their culture does in many respects represent the peak of human achievement; and to the extent that it is now threatened by barbarian forces, both from within and without, it must replenish itself more vigorously at source. To counteract the deaths from warfare and disease that will soon reach dismaying proportions, to keep the balance of age groups from falling too heavily on the downward side of the life-curve, it is necessary to introduce a biological counterweight: more babies. The desire for children, the focusing of activities on the side of child nurture and development, are healthy responses to the dehumanizations and devastations that inevitably accompany war. It is only by a fresh mobilization of vitality that the Western peoples will be able to hold their own.

Let me sum up this preliminary statement. The end of the period of land expansion must be accepted; the balancing of local resources is a complementary process to the establishment of a balanced world economy; and the two go hand in hand. The end of the period of mechanical industrial expansion must likewise be accepted; it is the condition, as Mill pointed out, for distributing wealth more justly and for achieving a more varied and interesting and purposeful life. But if the irrational increase of population, as a pretext for stealing a neighbor's territory or enslaving his people, must be combated, a more orderly and socially valid stabilization of the population must be undertaken; so that the possibilities of parenthood and family life should not be divorced from the normal expectation of life for any group or region.

So far the end of the period of expansion has been recorded in blind, irrational maladaptations: in conflicts for territory and markets, like those taking place between Japan, China, and Russia in Eastern Asia; in schemes for merely pecuniary security to compensate for increasing unemployment; in efforts to stabilize through military conquest and the restoration of caste within and slavery without; in a blind sterility, accompanied by an enfeeblement of family ideals.

Our expansionist institutions have lost their reason for existence; hence a hollowness, a persistent air of unreality, about many parts of our existence which needed no explanation and no justification in the past. Now is the time to envisage and incorporate a fresh ideal of life, based on the premise of stabilization: a life in which the power-impulse will be subdued by a renewed life-impulse, in which the program of one-sided conquest and domination of country by country and class by class will give way to a world-wide co-operation on the basis of a common goal, shared by equals; a program under which the ends of life will not be sacrificed to a mechanical multiplication of the means of living.

Many of the ideals appropriate to a more stable civilization have long been in existence; others have still to be restated in fresh terms, or to be framed in view of new possibilities. For the animus of the expansionist period, though a dominant one throughout Western civilization, was never entirely accepted. The early Christian ideal of the cultivation and salvation of the individual person was out of harmony with the motives of the conquistador and the capitalist; the world-wide religious concentration on the values of the inner life was always in conflict with the externalism and mechanism of the power-civilization. In the very heyday of expansionism, the middle of the nineteenth century, scarcely a voice could be found to defend either the means or the ideals of this power-civilization: Ruskin, Morris, Arnold, Emerson, Whitman, Thoreau, Dickens, Zola, Kierkegaard, Tolstoy, Nietzsche—all the representative minds of Europe and America, to say nothing of the cultures of the East, were revolted by the mythology of expansion: they protested against its inhuman sacrifices and brutalizations, its tawdry materialism, its crass neglect of the human personality.

But many plans that seemed like mere escapist dreams in the nineteenth century have become conditions for survival in our own age. It is only the attempt to live within the outworn shell of the past that condemns us to frustration, to sterility, to a savage barbarism. If we ask ourselves, not how to rebuild our metropolitan areas and keep our machines running when the war comes to an end, but how to keep life running, with or without the aid of machines, in or outside of our urban areas, we shall enable ourselves better to understand the conditions for urban and regional development that open before us.

6. LIFE IDEALS AND PRACTICAL PLANS

Such city planning as has existed during the last generation has started mainly from certain narrow physical, technical, and economic assumptions. The planner studied the site, made a canvass of industrial needs, measured the flow of traffic, and laid out plans for future roads or future water mains. One would have thought from the bulk of city plans, whether theoretical essays like Le Corbusier's or practical expedients like that of the local municipal engineer, that city life existed for the purpose of multiplying the mechanical means of existence. Even plans that stressed the idea of relationship, confined themselves, as a rule, to the physical terms of relationship: roads, highways, avenues, terminals, airports, shopping centers, factory districts.

In most countries, housing and city planning have been treated as separate departments of human effort. Yet even housing has taken place within the same general framework of ideas; most of the improvements in housing have been conceived in a purely mechanical fashion, in terms of experiments with materials and methods of building, of quantitative increase in equipment, of cheapening costs so as to make housing economically more available to lower income groups. As a result, the design and layout of the latest Federal housing development in the United States show no substantial improvement over the design and layout of the housing of the mill workers in Lowell, Massachusetts, more than a hundred years ago. Nothing has changed because the ideal behind housing has not changed; the workers' life in mill, office, or factory is still taken to be the central term of his existence; and improvement in the form and layout of dwellings is still conceived in mechanical or economic terms, not social and personal terms.

Now, just as our age has already seen, although mainly in a base form, the subordination of economics to politics, so it must see, in the transition to a more stable order, the subordination of the machine to the human personality, and economic needs to social needs. The technical and economic studies that have engrossed city planners to the exclusion of every other element in life, must in the coming era take second place to primary studies of the needs of persons and groups. Subordinate questions—the spatial separation of industry and domestic life, or the number of houses per acre—cannot be settled intelligently until more fundamental problems are answered: What sort of personality do we seek to foster and nurture? What kind of common life? What is the order of preference in our life-needs? Do we place babies above motor cars or vice versa? Do we place schools staffed by able teachers above schools that have expensively equipped shops and laboratories, gymnasiums and swimming pools? Or, even more fundamentally, do we want schools or do we want clover-leaf road-junctions?

Most of the current answers to these problems are evasions. It will not do to answer that we want everything; for even in the pre-war years, budgets were not illimitable. Countries that chose to be well-equipped for war, like Nazi Germany and Soviet Russia, forwent desirable consumers' goods; cities that spent their income and borrowed their capital to make vast physical changes, like the Wacker Drive in Chicago that cost a million dollars a mile, often failed to pay their teachers promptly or failed to build enough schools. The key to all intelligent spending was long ago laid down by Emerson: spend on the high levels and save on the low levels. But just the opposite principle was introduced by the age of mechanical invention, which spent recklessly on mechanical utilities and the preparatory functions and was reduced to penury or parsimony in providing for non-mechanical, non-profit-making activities—and therefore deprived itself of art and love and leisure, except in commercialized forms.

Nor can the problem of what sort of community, what sort of personality, we seek to produce be glibly set aside with a reference to the undoubted existence of individual differences. Different races, different nations, different regions, different temperaments and occupations, all have many minor differences in their needs: who would doubt it? But there is also in every age a common ideal of personality which represents the goal of living toward which everyone is more or less set. To the extent that an individual shares this personality, he is in harmony with his fellows and capable of making the fullest use of their common culture. The Protected Man of the Middle Ages was at home in his walled city; the Exploratory Man, the conquistador and the pioneer, felt at home when his vision could move unblocked toward the horizon; each of these modes of expression was the outcome of the dominant ideology, first Christian, then capitalist. The ideal of personality must be organically connected with the needs of the historic moment in which it lives. Neither Jacob

Fugger nor Captain Cook, neither James Watt nor Daniel Boone, neither Karl Marx nor Nicolai Lenin, gives an indication of the ideal type we must create for an age of stability. If the era of stabilization is to be one devoted to the intensive but balanced cultivation of our natural and human resources, balance and intensity are equally, I believe, the key to the sort of personality that is needed to work effectively within this culture and to create the necessary changes in our institutions. The age of mechanical specialization produced a quite different ideal: that of the one-sided specialist, supremely skilled in some fragment of human activity, but incapable of attacking life at more than one point. Outside the realm of occupational competence, the personality was badly organized and unintegrated, dispersed, the passive victim of outside stimuli, without an authentic center or a robust inner life.

Specialization, one-sided development, the unrelated pursuit of power and wealth, the unresisting assimilation of trivial and fashionable goods, produced merely for the market, were the typical requirements for personal success during the period of expansion; particularly, they became marked during the closing decades of this period. Hence a separation of the intellectual and the emotional sides of human life; hence further the emphasis on the impersonal, leading to callousness, and the final tendency to react against the loss of feeling and emotion by the ascendancy of the anti-personal, taking the form of mass brutality and sadism, in over-compensation for a growing sense of personal inferiority on the part of the masses. What is the cult of power, in its perverted fascist mode, but a final expression of that resentment against Man's impotence to control the external forces that threaten him?

The task for our age is to decentralize power in all its

manifestations and to build up balanced personalities, capable of utilizing all our immense resources of energy, knowledge, and wealth without being demoralized by them. Our job is to repair the mistakes of a one-sided specialization that has disintegrated the human personality, and of a pursuit of power and material wealth that has crippled Western man's capacity for life-fulfillment. We must provide an environment and a routine in which the inner life can flourish, no less than the outer life; in which fantasies will not be wholly dependent upon the film, in which the need for song will not depend wholly upon the radio or the gramophone; in which men and women will have a going personal life that is central to all their associated activities. We must create conditions of living in which the life of a parent will be as momentous and as full of interest and as valid as any other sphere of activity: a life with its own center of gravity. We must offer more physical outlets, not merely for aimless play, but for sober manual activities: the work of the gardener, smith, carpenter, weaver, no less than potter, painter, or sculptor. Ironically, the introduction of these salutary arts is now delayed until a neurosis appears; whereas in a well-balanced life they are ways of guarding against a breakdown. All these needs must be expressed in our designs and embodied in our structures.

In short, the ideal personality for the opening age is a balanced personality, one that is in dynamic interaction with every part of his environment, one that is capable of treating economic experiences and esthetic experiences, parental experiences and vocational experiences, as the related parts of a single whole: namely life itself. The importance of emphasizing the needs of variety and flexibility will come out more clearly, perhaps, if we call to mind the patent dangers that will attend stabilization itself: dangers that are already visible.

Organizations that have been stabilized for any length of time—the army is an excellent example—become embedded in routine and hostile to change. Scientific advances do not radically alter this fact, for they themselves tend to follow stable institutional patterns and tend to perfect themselves more and more within an obsolete frame of reference. Stability and security, pursued for their own sake, will result in a caste division of labor; unless shaken by some outside force, these caste divisions harden and the capacity for adaptation disappears both in the individual and in the organization as a whole. There are plenty of signs of this form of stabilization in present-day society; they have been seized upon, by Nazi philosophers and leaders, as the basis for permanent caste divisions.

It is precisely because stabilization carries with it this danger that we must introduce, into our conception of the type of personality needed, the ability to touch life at many points, and by continued reaction and interplay, break up the tendency to fall into a single fixed mold. In this respect, the varied war experiences that every part of the British and Russian populations has undergone, as soldiers, sailors, air raid wardens, fire fighters, nurses and so forth, must be regarded, in their peaceful equivalents, as normal requirements for a period of stabilization. Plainly we cannot afford to create a war every generation in order to break into fixed routines, to disrupt sessile habits, to renew our emotional vitality and recover our animal sense of alertness. We can and must, however, arrange our environment and our course of life so as to prevent premature fossilization—even those forms of it associated with expertness and professional skill. Individuality and initiative, to this end, must be divorced from their historic connection with private capitalism; they must be fostered, as counterpoises, precisely at the moment that collectivism triumphs.

A balanced personality may be defined as one capable of making the most out of every part of his organic and spiritual capacities, so as to be ready to respond effectively to every demand of life, and to nourish all his own life-needs with energy drawn from every part of the personality. The ideal of balance is very close to the Greek ideal of the Golden Mean in conduct; and even of the Renaissance ideal of the gentleman. But in terms of the age we face, it means a capacity for self-fulfillment and social co-operation that do not depend, as in Greece or in the Renaissance, upon the existence of large private wealth or of slave labor. To achieve balance, a variety of occupations, a variety of environments, a variety of social groupings must be open to the individual—not to encourage restless, uneasy dabbling in this or that activity, but to permit a periodical shaking up of routines. To make up for a loss of highly specialized skill, there must be increased capacity for adaptation. To make up for a single-track concentration, there must be range of vision and comprehensiveness of understanding.

These conditions are not impossible of fulfillment: they were partly present in England in the sixteenth century, and account for the great outburst of energy in every department of life during the Elizabethan period; they were present again in the United States during the first half of the nineteenth century, and they help to account, not only for great pioneer types like Audubon and Lincoln, but likewise for the fact that a pencil maker and surveyor was a great moralist, and a sailor like Melville became a superb imaginative writer. Balance by its nature is precarious, both in the life of the person and the community: hence it must be perpetually recovered, perpetually renewed.

Adventure no longer lies in extensive exploration but in intensive cultivation; it is in the spirit of Thoreau, not the spirit of Pizarro, that we must explore and conquer, not the lower races but our lower selves, not the wide ends of the earth but that part of the earth which embraces our regional community. In this new effort, we shall be closer to a universal culture, in which all men of good will may participate, than we were at any moment during the last four centuries, when we were opening up the world to Christianity and physical science by means of gunpowder and strong liquor.

In the interests of balance, we must look forward, as Sir Thomas More did in his Utopia, to an alternation of rural and urban occupations; in re-establishing this claim at the end of the nineteenth century Peter Kropotkin was on firm ground. We must expect more manual work from the intellectual, in order to keep him whole and sane and grounded in reality; and we must also expect—at whatever cost in intellectual blisters—more intelligence and intellectual effort from the rank and file of humanity, who have often slothfully sought to escape the responsibility for a more active and responsible political role.

This effort to achieve balance, from every side, is essential to the creation of a common world, more orderly, more harmonious than was Western society even in the nineteenth century. Finally, if the community is to achieve balance, this must be effected by counterbalancing all our impersonal, scientific conquests and our mechanical command over the environment by an ever deeper exploration of man's feeling and emotions, by a readiness to accept as real and valuable, not only events that can be reduced to a mathematical order, but the whole obscure inner world of the personality, with its desires, its dreams, its projections, its insurgences, its arts. The importance of providing for our subjective life has been forgotten in our planning, though the need for solitude, for withdrawal, for what is expressed, historically, in the cloister, is a basic one. Yet there is not a village or a housing estate that is well planned unless it has made provision for places of withdrawal—solitary walks, devious woodland paths, unfrequented towers, hard to climb—no less than places where people can gather together in groups for social communion or common recreation. The whole tendency of our mind, during the period of mechanical expansion, was so opposed to this need that the ideal of almost all planners is to make all places equally accessible, equally open, equally public.

In short, the balanced personality needs a balanced en-vironment to support it, to encourage it, to give it the variety of stimuli and interests it needs in order to grow steadily and to maintain its equilibrium during this process. In purely urban terms—hence *un*balanced in terms of man's fuller life-needs—the great metropolis provided this essential vari-ety for man's occupational, professional, and political inter-ests; and because of that fact the metropolis has played an indispensable part in the human economy since the seven-teenth century. Now that the metropolis can no longer serve the new economy, except by helping to direct in the decen-tralization of its own power and authority, we must utilize the organizing and planning ability of the metropolis to achieve a much more comprehensive balance. In the trans-formation before us, even in the smallest unit, we must seek to assemble all the invisible and visible elements that are necessary to ensure balance. The principle of the electric grid must be applied to our schools, libraries, art galleries, theaters, medical services; each local station, though producing power in its own right, must be able to draw additional power, on demand, from the whole system.

This image, incidentally, is a useful one to carry in mind in order to have a concrete picture of the difference between a metropolitan and a regional economy. Those who still cling to metropolitan traditions see the alternative distribution of population, energy, and the social heritage as a reversion to a crude and more self-contained economy; they have an automatic association between physical congestion and social wealth, and do not see how it is possible to tap this wealth without heaping it together in a single dominating urban pile and keeping it there.* In terms of the past, their love for the metropolis is not altogether unjustified. What they forget is that social forces which were available only by congestion before 1880 can now, in the twentieth century, be mobilized by our rapid means of communication and transportation, without their having to be inertly massed in a single place. Our system of distribution for electric energy is also a model for our social activities; and the resulting pattern is as much in advance of the metropolitan massing and congestion as that was in advance of the isolated industrial slum of the eighteenth century.

The great difference between the metropolitan and the regional systems of distribution is that the first is, by its nature, anti-rural, and therefore partial and lopsided and humanly deficient, while the regional system provides a place for every manner of human need. Physical decentralization, however, without the political and social organization that must accompany it, is open to the objections that the exponents of metropolitanism cast at it. Long ago, Sir Ebenezer Howard called attention to this. At no point in this paper,

* See for example an article by J. M. Richards, Towards a Replanning Policy, in the Architectural Review (London), July 1941.

indeed in no published work of mine, have I ever advocated mere physical decentralization. That has been fostered by those who have been unwilling to embark upon the large-scale social effort and the profound political reorientation that are necessary for effective community building and regional development.

7. PRIMARY ORIENTATION: THE FAMILY

So far we have been talking about balance in large and general terms. It is now time to talk about the personality and the community in relation to the special environments that exercise a deep influence on their growth and their ultimate form. The household and the region, the small intimate unit and the broad, all-embracing one, are the polar extremes of planning. If we can define their nature, their function, and their influence successfully, we will throw a light upon all the intermediate phases of living and planning. And first the household.

The human personality is formed, primarily, through the family. Philosophers from Plato to Fourier, from Engels to Bertrand Russell, have challenged the role of the family, because of its narrowness, its exclusiveness, its partiality; even Jesus said plainly that the family hampered man's higher vocation— "Woman, what have I to do with thee?"—and Paul gave it only a grudging recognition which was little better than downright dismissal. Because the break-up of the family into irresponsible individual units favored the use of its separate members competitively in industry, the last century has seen the household degenerate into a dormitory. This development had a far more searing effect upon the constitution of the family than all the criticisms and defamations of the philosophers. Except on farms, the family no longer has any collective economic task.

Is this situation destined to continue indefinitely? The answer is No. If the conditions that have prevailed in England and America during the last forty years continue for even another generation, the result will be wholesale devitalization and collective suicide. If the will to live prevails, a new cult of the family will restore it to a central place in our economy and our culture; the family will play a more conscious and purposive role in the nurture of its members; and the whole "problem of housing" will be stated in quite different terms.

With the expansion of mechanical industry the family functions, both immediate and remote, were dwarfed. Remoteness of the dwelling house from the workplace made it less possible for the family to meet as a unit even for meals; lack of sufficient dwelling space has made it difficult for members to escape being under each other's feet, even when they do come together. As the mechanical utilities within the house have multiplied, living space has shrunk. Lack of spatial separation between parents and children curbed the sexual life of the older generation almost as much as physical exhaustion; or forgetfulness of the need for privacy in sexual relations caused neurotic disturbances, as Freud demonstrated long ago, in the young.

While the dwelling house has become more sanitary, more mechanically adequate, there has been no commensurate expansion in our living quarters, such as took place after the seventeenth century in the accommodation of the middle classes. Quite the contrary: the expense of our accessory mechanical utilities, piping, paving, sewage disposal, has increased so far, in America at least, that it is roughly true to say that one room is buried in the street. This curtailment of living space has sometimes been excused as inevitable with the coming of the small family, in which the mother no less than the father is a potential breadwinner, who spends less of her time in the house. But the small family is a result no less than a cause. On the lower income level it is a result of insecure employment conditions or inadequate wage-rates based on the support of bachelors. On the upper levels, it is due to a desire for expensive comforts and luxuries and a fashionable routine of "conspicuous waste."

All over the world, millions of women have been driven to take jobs outside the family and to renounce the responsibilities and pleasures of domesticity in favor of a biologically sterile existence. The family as such was disparaged; the office and the factory became emblems of woman's emancipation—that is, of her sexual deprivation and her biological futility. Because of this, all the functions of the household have been progressively relegated to the care of paid professionals: from education to cooking, from preserving to nursing. This shift was hard for the individual to resist because it was identified with the new, the progressive, the enlightened; but it came, as a matter of fact, as the result of our decadent financial culture, and it repeated a development that had long before undermined the proud republic of Rome. The ideals of a pecuniary and power culture, which have dominated the world since the period of Western expansion, bear little relation to the constant demands of human existence. One of these primary needs is the need of reproduction: the personal need for love and sexual intimacy, the racial need for children, bred in an environment favorable to their physical and psychological growth; that is, the stable, reassuring environment of home and garden and nearby countryside.

One has only to examine the general pattern of city growth during the past century to discover that the mass of our urban areas were constructed with no thought for the central biological needs of the family. Even the upper-class suburb showed only a partial recognition of their place and importance. Nothing displays that fact more clearly than the threatened shortage of births: a shortage which indicates in England a probable recession of the population by 1970.* This is not stabilization but biological decline. It indicates that the middle-class standard or way of living is inimical to the needs of life.

This fact has a very direct bearing on all post-war planning. We must think, not simply in terms of industrial rehabilitation but biological survival; and to ensure survival we must give time and thought and money and love to the culture of the family. The family must have the essential space and equipment it needs, even if this means a radical diminution in profits or a complete socialization of building land. To put it crudely it would be better to survive in darkness than to die with the assistance of an electric light. Not, I hasten to add, that this is the actual alternative.

The household has now three primary functions: physiological, social, and educational. Physiologically, it is devoted to the repair, recuperation, and the replenishment of the human body. Within the same general biological frame, it is the most common meeting place of the sexes, for companionship, for recreation, and for procreation. Socially, the household is a means of association for diverse age groups; and with the development of the radio, the telephone, and the gramophone, it is the local center of recreation and amusement. As a family repository, the older form of household, with its space for storage, was an essential link in family continuity; it may well become this once more. Educationally, the household is the chief place of nurture for

* See Current Trend of Population in Great Britain, H.M. Stationery Office, 1942.

the young: particularly before the age of six. Economically, this is the place where accessory crafts, like knitting
and gardening, may be practiced both for the sake of individual satisfaction and collective support. By its variety of
functions, the dwelling house at its best contributes to the
balance and stability of its members: both as concrete fact
and as ideal symbol.

An age that has lost these family roots attempts to find
a degraded substitute in spectatorial sports and collective
manias; it creates and purchases complicated mechanical
toys to fill an irresponsible, vacant life in which family tasks
have little part; it breeds dogs, not babies, because they are
cheaper to maintain, easier to house, and more gratifying to
the owner's unqualified vanity. In order to give the family a
large role once more, in order to provide the household with
its most essential elements, land and domestic living space,
it may be necessary to simplify many other parts of our lives
and do without many of the pre-war essentials. Britain's experience of deprivation during the war will, I have little
doubt, make it easier to recover its general grip on reality:
no small compensation for what it has lacked and what it
has suffered. But every other country must learn the same
hard lesson. Only life is precious; machines, possessions,
utilities, comforts, are useful only to the extent that they
actively promote life. In the past, they have too often played
the role of a substitute.

The planning of a life-centered environment for the family
is the primary task in urban rehabilitation. When a choice
must be made, it is better to have the essential elements for
family living, combined with relatively primitive accommodation, rather than to have the last refinements in technology,
the electric refrigerator, a constant supply of hot and cold
water, fireproof construction, without the space and privacy

a family needs. During the transitional period from war to peace this choice may often condition not only the how but the where of building; and here the criterion should be plain: better incompletely equipped dwellings on the right pattern and in the right place, than fully equipped permanent dwellings that automatically continue the wasteful and sterile activities of the age of expansion. In England, this will mean giving priority in planning and building, not automatically to the places that have grown most in the past, or have suffered most from aerial attack, but those that promise most for the future. To qualify for priority, the traditional center must plan, not for superficial reconstruction, but for a profound renewal.

It is absurd to suggest that an adequate standard of family accommodation cannot be established after the present war because of economic difficulties. Particularly is it foolish to suggest this on the ground that urban land values, in terms of past uses, make it impossible to build housing for the common man except in high building blocks. It is the land values, or mechanical extravagances, that must fall, not the family dwelling standards. This is all the more necessary because in the post-war readjustment the fullest provision must be made for satisfactions and delights that do not depend strictly upon money income: the more parsimonious the physical existence, the more need there is for social and esthetic satisfactions in which purchased goods form a smaller part. No family can be treated as a wholly self-sustaining unit, whether culturally or economically; and this is not demanded. But with adequate domestic space, a family can be more self-sustaining in every sense than is possible in cramped quarters. The sky is no substitute for contact with the earth, and a view to look at does not take the place of a garden to work in.

To plan adequately for the dwelling house, however, one must plan at the same time for all the communal institutions and functions which enable people to do in larger groups what they cannot perform as families; these communal functions cannot be conceived as afterthoughts. More and more in our time collective wealth takes the place of individual wealth; the library, the art gallery, the school, bring to the poorest family resources which even the wealthy can hardly afford. If a play room for children is provided within a neighborhood unit, a group of intelligent mothers may take turns in supervising it; if the playroom is unrelated to the houses, so that access to it is inconvenient, it must be turned over to a professional worker, or it will be neglected. This holds for many other activities.

To scale down the costs of upkeep, we must rely more and more on voluntary services, performed in leisure time, as part of the collective responsibilities of each household. The care of parks and wayside plantations should be the work of school children. If we are to emerge from the present war without slumping to the defeatism and indifference that followed the last war, the tradition of energetic public service must be applied to peacetime civic activities. In the effort to achieve simplification, economy, and balance, work must be done by citizens that was once undertaken by paid officials— or not undertaken at all. What Victor Branford called "the resorption of government" is an essential part of the transition to a post-war, post-expansionist society.

8. THE REGIONAL PATTERN

If the first place to achieve balance is in the family, where the human personality is nurtured, the co-ordinate pole of planning is the region, for it is against the natural setting of hill and river and sea, of soil and climate, of natural formations and man-made landscape, that the human community defines itself. Geographers and sociologists have reached no unanimity in defining the region; and their failure is due to the fact that they are seeking to discover, by abstraction and definition, something that is a complex product of varied, never-ending natural and human processes. Nevertheless there is one characteristic of a region that must underlie every geographic or historic reference: it must combine the primeval, the urban, and the rural as part of the daily setting of life.

Sky, mountain, ocean, and river are part of man's constant environment; they form the elemental basis of our animal existence; they were associated with man's history, with his thoughts, long before he uttered an intelligible sound or learned to keep a fire burning. No urban existence that pushes the primeval background out of sight, that makes it remote and unavailable, that deprives people of intimate contact with it, hunting, fishing, rambling, exploring, collecting, boating, is likely to produce adequate men and women, able to cope with the realities of life and death. The coalescing of urban communities into one vast man-hive, a tendency to which Patrick Geddes gave the deservedly ugly name of conurbation, cannot be treated as a permanent urban phenomenon; it is a sign of that lack of political discipline which precedes and announces decay.

Those urban sociologists who cheerfully predicted that the population of the world would be sucked into such conurbations, did not reckon with the human cost of this development. Without contact with his primeval background, modern man tended to lose his sense of the ultimate realities—including all those obdurate conditions that lie beyond his technical improvements and his administrative contrivances.

No less needful for a sound urban life than the primitive background is that part of nature which has been tamed and ordered by man: the countryside with road and field, with orchard and garden. Relying upon trade with near and distant countrysides to supply its cities with the vegetables, the cereals, even part of the beef it needed, Great Britain permitted the land itself to be only partly used for agriculture; and unbalanced metropolitan regions, in every part of the world, followed this example. This undermined many more things than the food supply. For the countryside is not only a producer of food but a breeder of men; the routine of rural life, with its animal husbandry, its contact with all forms of life, its simple round of pleasures, is kinder to life than the best of cities, with every hygienic device, every form of medical care, that may be available. The birth rate is one index of this vitality; the mortality tables are another. In each case the countryside, even in poverty and ignorance, tops the city. In England the country squire, the clergyman, and the peasant have the longest expectation of life.

Regional planning, accordingly, must not merely be devoted to maintaining open land; it must be zealous to keep the countryside as an active, dynamic element in city life, growing food close to the urban market, because fresh foods offer most nourishment, drawing on the urban population for extra hands at harvest, locating appropriate factories and workshops in the country for the sake of giving agricultural workers and their families a second or alternative occupation, making the land economically productive, by utilizing every natural resource—in order to make it also culturally productive. No plan for urban estates or for new towns which is drawn up without respect for the soil maps of the region, which ignores the need of maintaining every area of high agricultural productivity, which seeks to maintain connection with the big metropolis rather than the land itself, can be considered as adequate. Our biggest cities must, in future, be country towns.

Both the primeval and the rural areas must be united in a fresh regional design; integral to that design, but never dominating it or obliterating the regional background, are the cities themselves. Capital must be made available for industrial and agricultural development, for building electric power lines, for harnessing water, coal, or sunlight, for promoting or relocating industries, if our plans for housing are not to repeat the stereotyped patterns of the past.

In other words, housing and community planning are not functions that can be undertaken by separate municipalities, acting within their own borders, seeking to deal superficially with effects of forces over which they have little or no control. Post-war housing programs, for both England and the United States, must avoid the mistake of doing over again on slightly improved lines something that ought not to have been done in the first place—or that ought to have been done in a radically different fashion. It is not simply "housing" that we must create, but a new frame for domestic and regional life. To continue our past forms would be to undo all the potentialities of the future.

In short, we must continually remind ourselves that the period of expansion is over and that the great urban masses created by that period are, in the nature of things, bankrupt; this war is the last declaration of insolvency. The mere massing of population and wealth no longer gives an indication of urban greatness; just the contrary. We have the task of giving form and character to a new period in the world's history; we must provide the stage and the setting for a fresh drama. What we conceive and do in terms of the past, though it be accompanied by the most refined technological improvements, is already obsolete. What we conceive and do in terms of the future, though we have only primitive means, will in time gather to it the energy and love that will produce greater works of collective art than those produced in the past.

Good planning, in the post-war age, will rest on the solid foundations of the family and the region; it will emphasize the biological and the social needs of the people, and it will treat industrial and financial needs as subordinate ones. It will be less afraid of the primitive than of the over-sophisticated; it will distrust what is overgrown, mechanically complicated, given to technical over-refinement; it will be as reluctant to build subways and mammoth transportation networks as the population of sixth-century Rome was to build new baths and amphitheaters. I do not by this mean that we have already regressed such a considerable distance toward the Dark Ages: indeed, I mean just the opposite, for by energetically commanding the forces of life, while there is still time to marshal them and deploy them, we may be able to avoid—as the Romans were not—the collapse of our whole civilization and the wiping out of its many grand and meaningful achievements in the arts and sciences.

But the watchwords are stability, not expansion: human culture, not simply mechanical progress. That imposes a new scale of values. Our too masculine, too mechanical, too life-denying society has come to its terminus. Perhaps the best slogan for the coming age is that for the lifeboats: women and children first.

THE PLAN OF LONDON

In the autumn of 1943 the editor of the Architectural Re-
view in London asked a group of American planners, archi-
tects, and critics to comment upon the plan prepared by
Messrs. Abercrombie and Forshaw to guide the London
County Council in the rebuilding of London.

The pressure of my own work on The Condition of Man
kept me from writing the brief criticism the Review had
called for; and when I finally put my hand to the task I
found myself in the midst of a large-scale job for which
neither the editor nor myself had bargained. My long-
established respect for Patrick Abercrombie's work, which
goes back to his East Kent and Deeside reports, gave me a
natural bias in favor of his Plan for London; but in spite of
its many high qualities both in the technical and the social
side of planning, I discovered, to my regret, that I could not
accept its underlying premises.

When I reached this conclusion I threw aside all detailed
comments on specific proposals, tempting though it was to
add either re-enforcements or counter-suggestions, and con-
centrated upon the fundamental matter that had been neg-
lected: the relation of population growth to city design. This
is a very complex matter for analysis, it goes without saying,
and even the best students of population have been too en-
grossed with other matters to have worked out in sufficient
detail the complex correlations between the tables of births

198

and deaths on one hand, and the regional, occupational, and urban variables on the other. The evidence is still spotty, because it needs not merely better statistical records on the basis of comparable units—which nations plainly are not— but because it also needs detailed sociological investigation of the kind that Le Play made in classic form in Les Ouvriers Europeens, without however tempting a sufficient number of other investigators to follow his rigorous example. Lacking such intimate knowledge, indeed, the available statistics lose half their value.

Unfortunately, as the business administrator and the politician know, action must daily take place on insufficient evidence: if we waited to achieve scientific or academic certitude, we would lose more from paralysis than we would gain by the avoidance of error. Fortunately action in itself brings with it an inevitable train of corrections, and those of us who propose to correct the complex evils of metropolitan agglomeration by proceeding in the opposite direction toward decentralization, regional unification, and comprehensive international co-operation have plenty of ground for believing that the course we propose will not merely salvage what is valuable in our existing civilization but will keep it from fostering the processes of self-destruction.

Should the planners of the London County Council be embarrassed by these criticisms of their premises, they might well say in their defense that they will look in vain for any clear statement of my current position in The Culture of Cities. Their criticism would be just: for I, too, had accepted the complacent neo-Malthusianism of the twentieth century, based as it was on nineteenth century statistics; and though I had warned the Regional Plan of New York that the curve of expansion on which they had based their plans was subject to change without notice, I did not fully interpret the need for temporarily counteracting the sterility of most Western countries till I published Men Must Act in 1939, and backed it up further with Faith for Living in 1940. So unfashionable has this point of view become, that those who have urged the democracies of Britain and the United States to concern themselves with the quantity as well as the quality of their births have even been characterized as reactionaries, indeed as outright fascists, because of this advocacy alone. This perverse association of ideas was characteristic of the "corruption of liberalism" about which I wrote in Faith for Living: it surrendered to fascism not merely the capacity to take the initiative and the capacity to act, but even the capacity to reproduce one's own kind, thus giving plenty of ground for the scorn that Spengler had expressed for a poor-spirited democratic ideology.

Such shallow thinking, such cowardice, should not for a moment be confused with rational democracy: ideas do not survive by themselves; they require energy and vitality to keep them alive in the real world. Such different minds as those of Emile Zola and Theodore Roosevelt both expressed this point of view long before I did; and I could only wish that their essential sanity here had taken deeper hold upon the hearts and actions of our democratic contemporaries. The one-sided stabilization of population that has taken place in the last half century threatens the very existence of Western culture: that loss would impoverish the rest of the world no less than ourselves; and it is on behalf of the universal values of which we are co-guardians, not on behalf of any merely tribal sentiment for blood and soil, that I now place the problems of population at the very center of our plans for urban reconstruction.

Finally, a word to my fellow-countrymen. The criticisms I have made of the Plan of London not merely apply to cities like New York and Chicago and Detroit: they apply emphatically to the regions of our own Pacific Southwest and Northwest; for the tendency to concentrate population in centers like Los Angeles and Seattle will effectually rob those areas of the great potential advantages they now hold for the improvement of human life. Even the present upward movement in the birth rate will be effectually curbed within a generation if the tendency toward metropolitan agglomeration and the habits of life this fosters are maintained. To avert this, we will have to muster everywhere an urban and regional statesmanship, together with a capacity for devoted public service, that so far the Tennessee Valley Authority alone magnificently exemplifies.

[This essay was first printed in the Architectural Review, London, and was then issued in the Re-Building Britain Series, Faber & Faber Ltd., London.]

1. INTRODUCTION

Under any circumstances, the County of London plan would stand forth among the important documents of the town planning movement. But the tragic necessity that has made planning on a great scale imperative need not have summoned up a commensurate vision; and the remarkable thing about Messrs. Forshaw and Abercrombie's plan is that the physical immensity of the task has not obscured the human sympathy, the human insight, of the planners.

Regrettably, the planners have not fully lived up to their vision; on certain matters, indeed, the superstructure they have erected denies their fundamental convictions. But even when the planners have erred, they have done so out of love for their city and out of a desire not to lessen the number of Londoners. Those of us who have admired from a distance the fortitude and gallantry of this great urban populace are also tempted to pray that their numbers shall be increased, not diminished: so the world must honor the planners' impulse, even if a consideration of the larger issues prove that it is self-defeating.

Among the big cities of the world London cannot perhaps claim to be the most beautiful, the most efficient, or even the most dignified; but it is surely the most lovable and the men and women of London make it so. Millions of them have lived under sordid, sometimes brutal conditions, but they have not at bottom become brutalized. They still have some of the mottled innocence of Sam Weller, the moral tenacity of Meredith's Skepsey; in short, they are lovable. Perhaps they have actually been sweetened by their physical handicaps, like the survivors in a blitzed area. Such a city the planner improves at his peril: not entirely sure but that some of its finer human qualities have proceeded from the very conditions that cry, it would seem, for correction.

Before I discuss this planning report in the rigorous fashion its great qualities deserve, I should like to add my personal tribute to the spirit in which it has been written and to its numerous positive achievements. My copy is full of annotations, and the words, "admirable," "sound," "excellent," appear on almost every page. As one has learned to expect from any work with which Professor Abercrombie is associated, this report has the great merit of taking an extremely complex collection of data, reducing it to manageable proportions, using it as a basis for clear-cut and reasonable proposals that can be followed step by step.

These planners understand that a city is not a purely physical structure. They see that the city is an historic organization, almost an organism, rich in traditions, full of memories, guided by processes that are sometimes too obscure to be rationally analyzed or too subtle to be arbitrarily guided. Instead of flouting such traditions as Le Corbusier proposed to do in his ruthless geometric reconstruction of Paris, the authors seek rather to make use of London's past. They summon up borough loyalties almost as resolutely as did Adam Wayne, the Napoleon of Notting Hill—not, like him, to resurrect archaic costumes and moribund interests, but to revitalize the social order by which men live.

If any group of men were capable of planning single handedly London's future, it would be the County Council that has enlisted such able professional aid and that has been, within the limits laid down, so well served by it. But that "if" raises a doubt, and on inspecting the report carefully the doubt becomes a challenge.

At this point my all-too-brief eulogy must come to an end. For ultimately I must raise the question as to whether the London County Council, great as it is, has the power to prepare an adequate plan for the future of London. I must ask if a plan for London—or any other British city—can proceed without taking its place in a larger scheme of regional and national development. While many of the proposals in the L.C.C. Plan have permanent value, I must finally suggest that the most fundamental problems have been neglected, because the future of London has been looked upon as a matter for self-determination. As a series of well-organized planning schemes, the report is admirable. What is lacking is not planning skill but something that must precede it: urban statesmanship. In the haste to rebuild London, this plan might unfortunately serve to hasten its downfall and complete its destruction.

2. APPROACHES TO THE PROBLEM

Under the above heading, the London plan discusses three possibilities. First: "unrestricted planning." Such planning would follow the lines taken by the M.A.R.S. group, by considering the city as an abstract physical structure and changing every characteristic except the name. The L.C.C. planners wisely dismiss this possibility; yet perhaps they do so too completely; for when it comes to detailed planning of neighborhoods they fail to consider sufficiently the guiding lines provided by an adequate theoretic solution and have not fully availed themselves of the precedents for sound modern standardization that have been partly worked out during the last generation.

As opposed to "unrestricted planning," the L.C.C. approach has been based upon an "endeavor to retain the old structure, where discernible, and make it workable under modern conditions." Having decided upon this course, the authors have also decided to retain the existing population for the county at large: their proposal to remove half a million people from the center, so far from being a revolutionary one, would actually lessen the number that was thrown onto the periphery of London during the 1930's.

Now this effort to retain London's existing population was a major decision. The whole plan depends upon it: in fact, the whole plan falls by it. But one looks in vain for any discussion of the considerations that governed it, or for even a recognition of the fact that it is the most debatable assumption in the whole report. Is it possible that this decision was determined for the planners before they were even called in to make their survey and prepare their report? If so, it was still subject to criticism, for the first duty of the architect and planner—little though the schools of architecture may teach

it—is to scrutinize the program of his client and to make
sure that the client has a correct insight into his own needs
and has embarked upon an enterprise he is capable of carrying out.

Apart from the lovableness of Londoners, what reasons
exist for retaining in the county of London its pre-war population? Of political and economic motives there are many:
habit, convenience, inertia all tend to make any existing set
of institutions to perpetuate themselves, even after the original causes and motives for their existence have ceased to
operate. Plainly, an enormous amount of capital has been
invested in the mere massing of London's population: its
elaborate and efficient transit system, its sewers and water
works, a host of secondary service industries all depend for
their existence upon keeping up the population of London.

With these trades and industries and public works go the
rateable values that their presence maintains. The ability of
the London County Council to keep up its admirable educational and health services rests, in part, upon maintaining
congestion. In addition, the very human love of power and
prestige contributes to this decision: since the seventeenth
century the great capitals have monopolized the cultural resources that once were far more widely distributed and the
very conception of metropolitan greatness has been associated with purely quantitative estimates of population and
wealth.

Yet the pressure to maintain the physical greatness of
London works contrary to the desire to produce a more
liveable environment. Against this desire for mere numbers,
stand certain indisputable facts. First, inner London has been
emptying out since as far back as 1861, when Holborn
showed a decrease in population: even the County of London
has lost population to the outer London area; so that while

the population of the Home Counties has gone on massing
and congealing, London as a city has shown the same symptoms of blight and disorder and depletion that the great cities
have borne witness to all over the world. Merely to maintain
the pre-war population of London, Messrs. Abercrombie and
Forshaw have to reverse two tendencies: the original tendency toward an expansion which sacrificed the rest of Britain
to London's imperial monopoly, and the secondary tendency
to compensate for the disasters of this expansion by escaping
to suburban areas on the margin.

The planners of London are correct in thinking that the
time for urban stabilization has finally come. But they are
wrong in thinking that their plan for retaining the existing
population of London will effectually aid this stabilization:
it would rather, as I shall show later, continue to have most
dire results upon the whole population structure of Great
Britain.

3. THE THIRD APPROACH TO PLANNING

There is a third approach to the problem, which the authors mention only to caricature, and caricature only the
more easily to dismiss. This is what they call dispersal: they
refer to it in terms that make it similar to the half-baked
fantasies of certain American planners and industrial de-
signers, people who are so enamored of the devices of rapid
transportation that they would retain the center of the cities
only as a daily gathering place for business, pretty much
like the City of London itself, whilst every other function
would be dispersed over the wide landscape.

Conceived on those lines, "dispersal" is only another
megalopolitan attempt to simplify the problem of life in
cities by translating every element into purely physical or
technological terms. This particular approach was first

sketched out, I believe, by Mr. H. G. Wells, in his Anticipations: at bottom it belongs to the same order of thinking as
that which has already created the existing mesh of cumber-
some mechanical services. The only difference between this
method and the actual dispersal of pre-war London would
be in the degree of urban dilution that the motor car and the
airplane and the helicopter would make possible in the
future. No one who understands the role of cities in civilization could possibly look forward with approval to the extension of that process.

But in the next five lines in which this alternative is
broached and dismissed, Messrs. Forshaw and Abercrombie
mention quite another consideration. "Should we," they ask,
"agree with those sociologists and technicians who declare
that Megalopolis must end in Necropolis, killed by its own
atrophy?"

That is another question. And since I am one of those
sociologists, it is precisely at this point that I would halt the
authors and challenge them to re-examine their choice. Have
they perhaps not made it a little too peremptorily? Have
they been blind to the sights around them, or rather, blind
to their significance? Have they failed to read the handwrit-
ing on the wall for the reason that the wall itself has already
been bombed into rubble? Unfortunately, the bombing itself
points to the message.

When Sir Patrick Geddes generalized the development of
cities into three stages of growth, followed by three stages
of decay, it was open to his critics to say that this historic
summary was not necessarily valid for our own civilization.
Had we not possibly found a way out of that impasse through
the use of a science and a technics that no other age had
possessed? Perhaps the death of the big city was as avoidable
as the death of a modern child from diphtheria.

But however pessimistic and premature Geddes's summary might have seemed a generation ago, one must rather be struck by its extraordinary realism today. If anything, one is disturbed by the essential lightheartedness of his study of the growth of conurbations in Cities in Evolution: so deeply engrained in him was the hopefulness of the nineteenth century that, biologist though he was, he did not utter a sufficient warning against its biological and social consequences.

That optimism and that oversight should not be repeated in the present generation; for we have come face to face with the lethal end-products of megalopolitan civilization: the misuses of mechanisms, the de-humanization of personalities, and the actual breakdown or obliteration of even sound urban structures in the ferocious interchanges of totalitarian warfare. Only with sadness and extreme reluctance does one who has lived remote from the bombed cities of Britain remind the planners of London that every bombed area is *ipso facto* a Necropolis: where men once crowded together strange plants now grow and birds nest, precisely as if Bloomsbury were Baalbec. Necropolis in our time has become one of the consequences of "peace in our time." What was once prophecy is now history. And those who have stood up so bravely to the bombing itself must carry their courage one step further and face the meaning of this unrestrained orgy of destruction.

Is the present breakdown of our civilization an accidental fact? There is massive evidence at hand for thinking that it is not: some of that evidence I have endeavored to collect and interpret in The Condition of Man (New York: 1944). What we have experienced in the last thirty years has been repeated in each of the twenty other civilizations that Mr. Arnold Toynbee has analyzed in his A Study of History. At a certain stage in every civilization's development, the proc-

esses of expansion and conquest over-reach themselves: the
vital interests of man are set aside and his moral and political discipline become inadequate to control the forces that
are his to command. This failure to maintain the human
measure leads in time to social disintegration, marked by a
wholesale flight from reality, and it brings about a reliance
upon palliatives and evasions which only further hasten the
decay of which they are a grave symptom.

The uncontrolled growth of the big cities is as much an
anti-vital process as the uncontrolled destructions of totalitarian warfare: they are both symptoms of a deeper disorder.
In the new plan for London I find the same failure to come
to grips with reality that one finds in the political behavior
of all the democratic peoples—not least of course isolation-
ist United States—during the nineteen-thirties. And this failure would still be serious even if the war had not broken out
and even if obliteration bombing had not been practiced.

For the death of the overgrown city has been written in
two ways, and both spell the same word: Necropolis. Megalopolitan civilization itself on one hand fosters pathological
reactions in many areas that it touches: its machine-centered
economy is hostile to no small part of man's essential needs,
and even the deep vitality and tough humanity of the British
peoples have not been able to overcome that fact. Not accidental, but typical, were the reactions produced in the ugly
mind of Hitler by his experiences as an outcast in Vienna,
for the absence of organic groupings and effective fellow-
ships gives rise to a demand for mechanical compulsions and
unanimities; and normal impulses, suppressed and frustrated in Megalopolis, return in the form of collective aggres-
sions. What is the result? A totalitarian religion that de-
grades the personality: a totalitarian tyranny that violates
the most sacred attributes of civil life: a totalitarian war that

brings the whole process to its final consummation of evil. All these phenomena have their somewhat disguised counterparts in non-fascist countries.

Fortunately, even in the biggest of cities, there remains a large residue of deeply human impulses, welling up with each new generation of children not yet subdued to their social environment: hence Spengler's prediction of the abject cowardliness of the urban proletariat has proved flatly untrue, from Madrid to London; and hence, as I pointed out in the Culture of Cities, *the processes of renewal may even at a late stage of decadence cut short the downward movement and initiate a fresh cycle of development.* But such an initiative demands an effort as heroic and as drastic in its displacement of past interests and past routines as that required by war itself. The attempt merely to patch and repair the existing structure of society, under the illusion that its dominating forces are benign and are pointed in the right direction, can only lead to the extension of ruin. Everywhere that ruin has now become visible.

But totalitarian war is not the only lethal product of our megalopolitan culture. Even had "peace" prevailed, the growth of the big city was self-limited; for the same result would have been reached presently in a no less inexorable fashion, if over a somewhat longer period. We are faced with premature death as an end product and with death at the source by the increasing practice of sterility and by the shutting off of new births. The greatest nineteenth century achievement in mass-production, the mass-production of human beings, has come to an end.

The big city grew originally and continued to grow chiefly by immigration. Even now it remains the least successful environment for reproducing men. Despite the increase of sanitary services, hospitals, and clinics, despite the lowering of its infant death rate, the population of the big city cannot be maintained without a steady import of people from more fertile areas: even to maintain their existing population the distended city must deplete the hinterland of men.

Now two great facts about population growth must be borne firmly in mind. First: after corrections for age differences are made, the big city compares unfavorably with the small town, and still more with the open country, as an environment helpful to reproduction. The statistics on this are perhaps clearer in the United States than in England, because in the latter country a far higher degree of urbanization exists, and the entire country has been more deeply affected, over a longer period of time by the dominant metropolitan pattern. Second: there is a differential fertility between economic classes, with a higher degree of reproduction among the poor: so that any mere improvement in their economic well-being is not in itself likely—without a change in social customs and purposes—to raise the birth rate; on the contrary, it would probably tend to lower it further.

Under present circumstances, the greater the portion of a country's population that is retained in big cities, the surer becomes its biological doom. That is what one means when one says that the growth of the big city is self-limiting. Megalopolis is both a symptom and an instrument of biological failure; and it is perhaps no accident that the first city of this name was established on "modern town planning lines" precisely in the age of decadence in Greece, by deliberately moving the population of the surrounding villages into a single center. Even in the United States, with a larger rural population than England, the continuance of the big city in its present form must be viewed with unconcealed alarm: but in England the danger is more critical because of the higher degree of general urbanization and by the relatively small margin of difference between the rural and the urban net birth rate.

With the rural reservoir of population falling, London faces a shortage of inhabitants. This can be overcome only by depopulating the rest of Britain. That is an urgent reason for re-building the city on lines that will make it once more an adequate biological environment. So far from taking advantage of that opportunity, the L.C.C. planners have ingeniously attempted to combat it. This effort has been fatal to most of their palpable good intentions.

Let us be clear about what is happening to London and indeed to urban civilization generally. The sterility of the big city is a purposeful sterility: it is due to the essential failure of this civilization to arrange the goods of life in a rational order, and to put biological and social purposes above those mechanical and financial achievements—with their complementary "diversions"—which have become emblems of megalopolitan success. The mischief is not due solely to the physical ills produced by a wasteful and overcomplicated urban routine: it is due to a growing concern for the inessential, the trivial, the glamorously empty, which Paul of Tarsus found, in a similar period of decay, among the Corinthians and Athenians. This wholesale perversion of values is fatal to life: as fatal if carried to the extreme as the demand of a starving man for cigarettes instead of for food. Any plan that accepts the current scale of values can only give a durable form to a widespread, though perhaps unacknowledged, death-wish. The forgetfulness of these essential biological facts has been partly responsible for the death of most past civilizations.

4. THE IMPORTANCE OF BEING BORN

How many people should the planners of London endeavor to retain? A short-sighted prudence, remembering the need for retaining the existing structure of land values and rates, would say: substantially all the pre-war inhabitants. But that answer is an arbitrary one. In terms of Britain's needs and responsibilities a more reasonable answer must be made: fortunately, it may be put with some precision. The present area of London County should hold no more people than will enable it to have a net reproduction rate of at least 1.0. The ability of any group or community to reproduce itself is a measure of its biological health. That answer should modify every detail of the planning.*

To achieve the net reproduction rate of 1.0 involves a very comprehensive program of institutional and personal changes, as Alva and Gunnar Myrdal have made plain in their examination of Sweden's parallel problem. These changes cannot be reduced purely to physical or environmental terms. And yet, within the wider processes of our civilization as a whole, certain urban patterns, certain densities, certain opportunities for human expression are plainly helpful to a high birth and survival rate, and certain others, we know definitely, are hostile.

When life is reduced to its lowest primitive level of eating, working and copulating the population will tend to rise: that is equally true on a Russian farm or in a London slum: hardship, desperation, and even brutal conditions tend, it

* "A net reproduction rate of 1.0" means a sufficient number of children in each generation to keep the existing population stable. Since many potential mothers die before achieving motherhood, since some remain unmarried, since others are sterile, and others have only one child, the average number of children per family must be over two in order for the existing population merely to hold its own.

would seem, to produce a compensatory vitality. *What are the equivalent conditions on a high level of culture?* That answer has not yet been satisfactorily made: the two Englishmen who attempted hardest to understand some of these conditions, D. H. Lawrence and Havelock Ellis, were handicapped by the nature of their own marriages and their personal failure in parenthood. But the Chinese and the Jews, those tough survivors of so many wornout civilizations, provide us with a real clue: parenthood itself must become a central interest and duty; and the family and the primary group of workfellows and neighbors must become a vital core in every wider association. The rural conditions of stability and continuity, the rural association with the facts of growth and reproduction, of life and death, must become an intimate part of the environment of the modern city—not restricted to mere week-end excursions and summer holidays, not thrust far out of sight and mind, like a suburban cemetery. Not least must we plan so that the rural sense of process, on which Miss Rebecca West has written,* will permeate our entire life, counterbalancing the mechanical tendency to make the process mysterious, the results magical, and the sense of personal responsibility quite absent.

The peasant, the shepherd, and the fisherman dare not lose this saving sense that life is important: life above all; so that they will forego comforts, forego security, even forego freedom of movement in order that the life-processes themselves shall go on. That sense of the importance of life is paradoxically fostered by war, not only in the soldier, but in every civilian who has actively participated in its hardships and duties, in rescue and salvage. But our cities have not been planned with any such insight or any such scale of values. Even our suburbs, no matter how open and green, only ac-

* Black Lamb and Grey Falcon. Viking Press. New York: 1941.

centuate in the routine they impose that contempt for vital
processes and that worship of the non-essential out of which
fortunes in gadgets and drugs, in trashy magazines and
brightly wrapped packages, have been made. Fortunately,
the terrible necessity that has made it imperative to cultivate
every square foot of soil in Britain has brought about an
at least temporary transvaluation of values. Every new plan
for city development should seek to conserve these values.

Two men above all others understood the vital promise of
modern civilization over a generation ago, and took steps to
transform our money economy into a life economy: Peter
Kropotkin and Ebenezer Howard. Those who assume that
their proposals have become out of date during the last
twenty years have not yet caught up with them; for nothing
should be plainer now than the fact that Garden Cities of
To-Morrow and Fields, Factories, and Workshops have laid
the foundations in thought for the approaching age of stabilization, of integration, of balance. The forms of industry
and agriculture, and the forms of urban living put forward
by these two thinkers are capable not only of neutralizing
the evils in our past civilization but of making the fullest
use of all the positive contributions of modern science and
technics. Howard's grand plans for canalizing the flow of
population, diverting it from the congested centers to balanced communities, his plan for decentralizing industry and
setting up both city and industry within a rural matrix, the
whole conceived on a human scale, is technologically more
feasible today than it was forty or fifty years ago; and the
need for such political action, in order to ensure survival, is
even more bitterly imperative.

Unfortunately, most of the current schemes for urban reconstruction rest upon the continued acceptance and further
projection of a pattern of life that was already obsolete and

inefficient, as well as sterile and inhuman, in Howard's and Kropotkin's day. For all their appearance of technical adroitness and formalistic modernity, such plans are really backward looking: filled with a smug, uncritical love for the dead forms of a mechanistic ideology. And despite their human interests, Messrs. Forshaw and Abercrombie have fallen into the same mechanical trap.

Now these considerations, remote though they may at first seem, have a direct bearing on the new plan for London. For nowhere have the authors asked themselves the fundamental question: What price must be paid in the re-making of London for the privilege of being born? If the people of England are willing to pay the price, London and England will survive—London with a smaller population, England with a bigger one; whilst centers like New York, which continue to pyramid their mistakes, will descend with Gadarene swiftness into the abyss. But if the price seems too high, as it may very easily seem in purely financial terms, then both London and England will dwindle; and the whole process of reconstructing London, even if physically achieved, will result in a magnificent—or perhaps not so magnificent—urban mummy, surrounded by a sumptuous tomb.

5. POPULATION AS *THE* URBAN PROBLEM

What I have said so far amounts to this: the conditions for London's survival, to say nothing of its re-building, do not lie primarily in the hands of the London County Council. But this makes it imperative for the Council to frame its program for reconstruction with a view to the larger whole, and to demand that certain great national decisions first be made, in order to lay a firm foundation for its own plans.

In a country whose net reproduction rate is so low that it threatens a considerable decrease of population by 1970, the failure to face the problem of population as an essential key to the correct design of cities is, quite literally, suicidal. This is not a matter in which any personal preference for existing land ownerships or high densities has any more validity than a personal preference for arsenic or carbon monoxide. If the biological problem of survival is not solved, the most elegant technological innovations, the most humane social provisions, will turn out to be frivolous diversions: diversions that kept people from facing their true plight: a final flight from reality.

So the great question that underlies the planning of London, and indeed every other urban center in Britain from Birmingham and Glasgow down, is just this: how completely must current megalopolitan standards of life be changed before the city becomes a favorable biological environment. That answer must be worked out experimentally. No one can yet say if two million or three million people must be emptied out of the present County of London area before the constituent boroughs become capable, severally, of reproducing their population from generation to generation. But one thing is sure: this end cannot be achieved by endeavoring to maintain most of the existing population, still less by doing this in schemes that raise the density of population in its central areas, by subsidizing ground landlords instead of fathers and mothers.

There is a school of planners who would solve the problem I have put by emphasizing and perpetuating the present difference between megalopolis and countryside. This school is represented by Mr. J. M. Richards, in his writings in the Architectural Review; and though I do not suppose Messrs. Forshaw and Abercrombie share his convictions I would anticipate such criticisms here and now. This school thinks of the metropolis as forming a special system of life, molded chiefly by forces and processes that operate over the entire planet, insulated from the countryside, the village, the region: insulated and essentially antipathetic. It would be logical for those who held such views to say that metropolitan sterility must be counterbalanced by rural fertility: let the country devote itself to breeding men and let the big city continue to consume them.

This was, in fact, the practical arrangement that held during the nineteenth century, before the habits and interests of megalopolitan civilization consolidated to form the dominant culture of our age. But the insulation which Mr. Richards attributes to the metropolis is a special historic phenomenon: a phenomenon based upon a one-sided exploitation of the many by the few, with the creation of an internal proletariat within the big city and an external proletariat, also exploited without mercy, overseas. Except when this decadent state has been created, the countryside has never been outside the currents of international life and the great city has never severed the umbilical cord that binds it to its hinterland. Take the handsome stone villages of the Cotswolds: these thriving villages and towns were a by-product of the international woolen trade; and the buildings of Burford and Bybury, for all their subtle regional flavor, were done in the international style of their period: a style visible with local variations in Oxford and Canterbury and Antwerp and Geneva. Mr. Thomas Sharp is correct in admiring the urbanity of the pre-industrial English village: that urbanity was the emblem of a common culture it shared throughout Europe with the biggest centers.

But the reverse process now holds. In our age, megalopolitan standards have become dominant; and the mode of life London has made fashionable dominates even the remotest country district, not merely because trippers and travelers bring these standards with them, but because the natives independently are seduced by them, since they breathe them in with their school education, with their newspapers, their advertisements. Hence the countryside itself now shows the same recession of population as the big cities: not so drastically perhaps but in the long run just as fatally.

Theoretically, London might hold its own by importing population from existing world centers of high pressure. But the decision of the 1906 elections over the importation of Chinese labor into South Africa should not give much encouragement to those who would maintain London's population by a similar method; and even were it instituted, it would hardly answer the problem of the British people's survival.

Within the British Commonwealth, the rural reservoir is running dry. If even the present population of Britain is to be maintained, the sterility of the big city must be overcome. And since Greater London contains almost one-quarter of the population of Great Britain, any plan for rebuilding a large part of this area, which ignores the basic facts of population, and fails to encourage fundamental changes in the life-aims of its citizens, must be condemned for its negligence of essentials. The complacent neo-Malthusian bias that still prevails is based upon nineteenth century population statistics; and we have still to cultivate a more reasonable attitude toward birth and survival, based on the statistics of the past thirty years.

In these facts and principles we have, then, a positive criterion for measuring any scheme of urban reconstruction Does it recognize the need for a life-centered environment? Does it make possible a biologically more satisfactory mode of existence than the megalopolis has fostered? If so, its foundations are at least sound; if not, then its foundations are shaky, and the possibility that the planners of London so glibly dismiss, that the "Megalopolis must end in Necropolis, killed by its own atrophy" will presently become an inescapable reality. For mark this: a plan may do away with traffic congestion, provide on a large scale for amusements and open air recreations, supplant every slum that needs demolition with a mechanically modernized group of flats, increase the provisions for sanitation and disease prevention and help lengthen the life of the existing population—and yet it may fail to encourage what is now a primary condition for the good life: the reproduction of children. The place where the great city stands, as Walt Whitman reminds us, is not the place of stretched wharves and ships bringing goods from the ends of the earth: it is the place of the best-bodied men and women.

Here I would turn against the Plan of London the Chinese proverb that Mr. Abercrombie has so effectively used as a preface to his excellent report on Plymouth. "If you are planning for one year, plant grain; if you are planning for ten years, plant trees; if you are planning for a hundred years, plant men." My capital criticism of the County of London Plan, is that in the very face of their own obvious sympathies and interests, the authors were not planning for a hundred years. Had they done so, they would have put men first. On the contrary, they were planning in the hope that they could somehow hold the pre-war population of London a little while longer, without disturbing drastically the conventions, economic, political, legal, social, that have been so steadily depleting the man-power of the country as a whole. They asked themselves, in effect, how far London must be changed in order to remain the same. And they forgot, when they asked that question, that if it actually could be made to remain the same it would, by that very fact, dwindle away, doomed by its sterility.

That dilemma is an inescapable one. On the willingness to face it and deal with it forthrightly the very survival of the British people, and incidentally the survival of these lovable Londoners themselves, depends. The heart of the Commonwealth and Empire is failing: and should it continue to fail the great polity it built up since the times of Elizabeth will vanish. But, just as in the formation of the British Commonwealth of Nations, England has effectively divided its power and dispersed some of its political initiatives in order to maintain the integrity of the whole, so in the case of London: that city must become less in order to become more. Much that London held merely by topographic monopoly must now become the equal possession of every other city and village in the kingdom. Here plainly the first shall be last; and the willingness to make this so will eventually save the first, too.

Behind this change is a fact that the admirers of megalopolitan concentration steadfastly refuse to face: the form of megalopolis has been made obsolete by modern innovations in swift transport and instantaneous world communication and the rapid manifolding of records. Under present-day technics, congestion is not a necessary condition for communication and co-operation. Even the inertia of a great past cannot maintain in indefinite existence a mode of life and a civic structure which fails both to satisfy our constant needs and to make the most effective use of our new instrumentalities. The smallest village is once more part of a whole that includes the world at large and all its varied resources; and the largest agglomeration must have within it, as a condition for survival, those fundamental sanifying contacts with earth and sky, those securities that are based, not on impersonal mechanisms but on the organic co-operations of parents and children, of household and neighborhood, which account for the continued survival of peasant stocks through all manner of natural and human catastrophes.

This does not mean that London should vanish: quite the contrary. Only the stubborn worship of London's dead self, only the desire to maintain an obsolete social and economic structure, will make its extinction inevitable. If on the contrary the will-to-live prevails, if the people of Britain are ready to stop at no measures that are necessary for the survival of all that is historically and socially important in London, then its dropsical organism may be drained and the city, reduced to a human scale once more, may start a new cycle of balanced development. But one outstanding fact must be frankly acknowledged: the Parasitopolis of the late nineteenth century has already become the spectral Necropolis of the mid-twentieth century. Every sound proposal for re-building and re-ordering London must recognize that grim fact and use every political and educational power the community possesses to circumvent it and triumph over it.

6. THE CONSEQUENCES OF INERTIA

Presently, I shall discuss further the political preconditions of re-planning London. Here I wish to follow out briefly the consequences of ignoring these preconditions and of complacently continuing those processes in modern civilization which have already brought us as close to wholesale disintegration as were the contemporaries of St. Augustine.

Let us ask, then, how the planners would deal with the reconstruction of Central London on the basis they have laid down for themselves. The chapter in which the basic policy is discussed is headed "Decentralization," but on examination this decentralization turns out to be so limited as to be unworthy of the name: what the scheme actually proposes is mainly a regrouping of population and industry within the London area. Out of the overcrowded center of London, the planners purpose to remove a mere five hundred thousand people. Does such an exodus give them an opportunity to provide enough open spaces, enough housing quarters that conform to family needs? Not at all: the park space provided for the inner ring of the city is not merely below any decent modern standard: it is below that which resulted from happy historic accidents in the West End. As for population, after the exodus has duly taken place, it leaves the planners providing a standard for the internal housing of London of 136 people per net housing acre; while admittedly they regard one hundred as desirable.

Both these standards of open space and density are arbitrary. What considerations governed them? First: inertia, the tendency to continue smoothly the past errors committed by the London County Council, particularly during the 1930's. Second: economic prudence and historic pride: the desire to retain most of the pre-war population within the existing county area. Third: the desire to frame a solution that made a minimum demand for national action: the five hundred thousand people they propose to remove represent the top number that would go with the amount of industry that— in the planners' words—could be *expected* to migrate. I underline the word expected; because if the desire for adequate standards were pressing enough, the number of industries that could be *persuaded* to leave London through the provision of more adequate quarters elsewhere and through a policy of controlled industrial decentralization, as proposed in the Barlow Report, is obviously far greater than any merely local effort could *expect*.

Failing to see that the problem demands a wider authority

than the London County Council can exercise, the planners have trimmed their standards to the Council's powers. In establishing this high density of housing they sanctify and enlarge the mistakes, like the White City at Hammersmith, that the L.C.C. has already made: mistakes calling for self-criticism, repentance, and correction. Instead of treating the relatively plastic situation, with the great demolitions of buildings, and the great displacements of population, as a means of making a fresh start, the L.C.C. proposes to act as if nothing had happened—as if the war itself, and all that it has revealed about the weaknesses of our civilization, were a wholly accidental phenomenon which called only for somewhat larger slum replacement schemes on the same model as the past.

Unfortunately, to maintain the density the planners propose is to maintain a corresponding scheme of life: a scheme in which it is easier to keep a dog than to raise a baby, in which one is more tempted to flee from the city on every possible holiday than to dream of enjoying the great social and cultural resources it actually possesses; in which the improvement of the housing conditions of the less skilled workers will only make them the victims of what Shaw's Dustman properly rejected: "middle class respectability."

In this scheme of life, the mechanical means of existence become ever more elaborate and compulsive, while the human ends are ever more remote and dim. In the human personality, "nature, habit, and reason" are divorced: the instinctual man, the social man, and the ideal man are set at odds instead of being reintegrated within the city on a higher level. Such an urban culture is equally far away from the basic realities of animal existence, with its alertness to danger and its allegiance to the needs of the group, and from the higher realities of the personal life, with its capacity for universal interests and for co-operation with groups remote in time and space. That devitalized culture almost willed its own annihilation when fascism threatened it; and there is little hope for a post-war world in which its ideals continue to exercise a dominant influence.

By the premises it has laid down, the Plan for London would consolidate what was weak in London's past and neglect certain very vital parts of that city's great traditions. What, for example, is the most important feature of London's housing, a characteristic that makes it so different from Berlin, Paris, Rome, Vienna, or Manhattan, a tradition deeply responsible for its essential humanness? Surely it is the fact that London is an open city; a city wealthy in open spaces and small houses, acre upon acre of park in Westminster, Bloomsbury, and South Kensington, mile upon mile of modest homes, standardized, often cramped, unfortunately not seldom sordid; but nevertheless built on a human scale, with just enough backyard space to make the care of little children pleasanter and easier. Humanly speaking, Mr. Wemmick's villa with its moat and drawbridge is not as ridiculous in terms of domestic needs as a ten-story apartment house. The Old Un's crotchets are essentially closer to man's abiding impulses than the modern rationalizer's calculations.

Who can doubt the sanity and wisdom of this original urban structure—one of low buildings, individual houses, and a private life counterbalanced by the amiable gregariousness of the street markets, the parks, and the pubs? Is it only a Dane like Rasmussen or an American like myself who beholds this characteristic fact of London's life and says: "*This* is London!" Surely not: the Londoners themselves, in common with all other Englishmen, are agreed about this: every survey that seeks to find out the preferences of the common man and woman in housing, reveals that they are overwhelmingly in favor of the single family house: even when the person who conducts the survey is, like Mr. Arnold Whittick, openly trying to prove just the opposite. Many Londoners are willing to put up with endless discomfort and tedious travel in order to provide individual houses for their families.

That tradition cannot be ignored on the ground that the Londoner has never seen a modern well-built flat with all its conveniences. With incredible obstinacy housing reformers, from my philanthropic compatriot, Peabody, onward have been presenting Londoners with model flats. The County Council itself has put up row upon row of these tall buildings, often handsomely designed and ably planned: the well-to-do middle classes, from Queen Anne's Mansions on, have lent to the mode all their prestige, even the holy name of Park Lane itself. And still the desire for the one-family house remains: even the boxlike caricature of that ideal produced originally by the seventeenth-century jerry-builder and standardized to its last degree of drabness and muddled insufficiency in the nineteenth-century bye-law street does not dampen that desire.

The saving life-sense of the cockney was never better illustrated than here, unless maybe in East London's summer pilgrimage to the hopyards of Kent. One would think that a tradition as deeply rooted as this would be respected in any plans for the future of London: it constitutes a basic human minimum. The real problem is to combine this desire for the one-family house with a modern neighborhood plan that will have no less spaciousness and beauty than Bloomsbury in the eighteenth century or Hampstead Garden Suburb in the early twentieth. It may be a little while yet before the future Londoner can make love to his wife in a summer house in his garden as William Blake, certainly no man of affluence, did; but that might at least be held up as an ideal, if we are as earnestly committed to the rehabilitation of family life as we ought to be.

It is, then, with surprise, indeed with dismay, that one finds that the planners of London have given little thought to the terms on which the one-family house may be rehabilitated. They have done just the opposite: the plans for re-populating Hackney, Shoreditch, Bethnal Green, contemplate making more than half of the new structures flats: some of them eight- and ten-story flats. It avails not that these flats will have "sufficient" open spaces around them or that their inhabitants will reach the upper floors on lifts: that does, indeed, distinguish these dwellings from those of Edinburgh or Glasgow; but it hardly makes any less serious the outright breach with an old and healthy tradition.

Whatever poverty England may encounter after this war, whatever burdens its reconstruction may impose, it cannot afford this kind of re-planning. Even if it were economically cheap, it would be humanly wasteful; and the fact is that—land values apart—it is the most extravagant method that could be applied. Even if London were to be made partly bankrupt through a loss of rates by an adequate provision of open spaces and family houses, the country could well afford to redeem that bankruptcy by reason of the annual flow of vital wealth it would be securing, in new citizens, keyed to live and love, to work and invent, to take over a larger range of political duties and civic tasks, by the fact that they at last had a city designed to satisfy the true needs of its citizens. There is no mechanical substitute for such an order, and there is no financial equivalent for the wealth it can produce.

If Messrs. Forshaw and Abercrombie's Plan defies the

tastes and traditions of London in reducing the proportion of single-family houses to apartments, it likewise falls short in setting a standard for open spaces. Whatever criticism one might make of the housing of the West End of London, one could at least say that its park spaces, thanks to the chain of royal parks, rounded out by the Thames and Chelsea Embankments, were near to a desirable level. Perhaps no parks in the world are better placed or more fully used than this beautiful central greenbelt. This system cries to be completed, not to be reduced.

But what actually does the plan propose? Because of the dismal lack of open spaces in the East End and most of post-Regency London, the planners put the standard at four acres per thousand inhabitants, with three more per thousand to be provided for Sunday use outside the County Area. For everyday use, then, four acres is the standard. This proposal is accompanied by many wise suggestions for retaining green wedges that surround London and opening much longer stretches of the river front for recreational uses. But instead of lifting London as a whole to the original level of the West End, the plan sets a low level for the city and then congests the West End parks by proposing to raise the density of population in that area to two hundred per acre. Here "expediency" has governed: but what kind of expediency is this that fails to take advantage of the opening up of London by the Blitz, and that governs its calculations by compromising with an undesirable past, instead of working toward a desirable future?

As to the immediate purpose that has made the Council planners decide to increase the density of population in Westminster and nearby areas—to enable a large number of people to live closer to their place of work and to decrease traffic congestion—I am naturally in complete agreement.

That end is desirable. But there are other ways of arriving at it than the planners have considered. If I mention them here it is only to point out how the planners, once they chose the path of congestion, automatically shut their eyes to other modes of development, even when they might have contributed to the very renovation of the constituent boroughs that they consciously favor.

The guiding principle of decentralized planning for industry is that the worker should not be too far separated from his work. Why should this principle not apply to the most characteristic work of London, that of government and business administration?

The piling of government offices in Whitehall and the neighboring areas has long passed the point where any efficiency is to be gained by it: not merely that, but the intrusion of big business into this area, as in the case of the great office buildings of the oil and armament corporations, is against public policy: if only because the pretentious buildings of these corporations, besides spoiling the river skyline, blotted out so much necessary housing space. If the City of London cannot hold such enterprises, the latter should have a place in the development that the Plan proposes for the South Bank.

Now I submit that any plans for re-grouping industry within London should begin with government itself: this should follow the internal decentralization of educational facilities that originated with the building of new museums and colleges in South Kensington. There are many great offices of government that need not crowd around Whitehall: functions that could serve and intercommunicate quite as well as they do at present if they were decentralized to their appropriate boroughs: the Colonial Offices to the neighborhood of South Kensington, perhaps, the Education Offices to

Bloomsbury, the Labor Offices to Battersea or Bethnal Green. Such a dispersal could be made without putting any office further away from the House of Parliament or any other office than thirty minutes by underground or taxi. The telephone and the pneumatic tube would bind such offices closer together for practical purposes than they were at the extremities of Whitehall up to 1890. Moreover, the diffusion of government workers as residents in these boroughs would create better balanced communities. Not least, it would combat that disastrous class segregation by boroughs which Shaw so devastatingly satirized in Pygmalion.

In all these criticisms, what I am proposing as an alternative is not contrary to the authors' declared intentions, but rather an attempt to suggest a more adequate scheme for carrying them out. For the governing insight of this plan, the basic idea which gives it vitality, is the "recognition of community structure." London's great effectiveness as a city, as a complex political and cultural organism, rests partly on the fact that it has escaped the disease of one-sided centralization and that it has not completely wiped out its constituent boroughs as either political or social entities. London is a federation of historic communities. With admirable insight the planners have proposed to emphasize these existing communities, "to increase their degree of segregation, and, where necessary, to reorganize them as separate entities."

In that statement the authors laid down the guiding lines for a truly great plan of London: one capable of surgically removing its undifferentiated cells and creating groups of organic communities, each with a balanced internal life, each a co-operating member in an interdependent and equally organic whole. Such a London would become in effect a constellation of garden cities, a "town cluster" in Ebenezer Howard's words; but it would have many definite advantages

over newer communities by reason of its historic momentum,
its political and cultural continuity. The restoration of the
human scale within the component parts of the present
County of London is a first step toward initiatives and co-
operations which will have to be carried on over a much
wider area than the County of London. As to the extent of
that wider area, one can perhaps get a rough view of its
nature by comparison with Holland: the one advanced country in Europe which has shown a reproduction and a survival
rate that compares favorably with peasant cultures.

Holland has almost the same population density for the
country as a whole as England and Wales: 687 per square
mile as compared with 668. *Greater* London has roughly the
same population as Holland; but Holland has eighteen times
the number of square miles. In this area, there is an almost
even balance between the rural and the urban populations.
Allowing for the special physiographic reasons for urban
density in Holland, and apart from the overgrowth of Amsterdam and Rotterdam as unitary cities, Holland presents
an adequate general pattern for both rural and urban development. Any plan for London that is framed in terms of
human welfare, must be on a comparable scale and must call
for comparable opening up of congested areas and a comparable development of agriculture within the greater regional unit.

Metropolitan London, even the County of London, is too
small a unit for re-planning and re-building, indeed, the essential provincialism of the metropolis is one of the chief obstacles to its reformation. If London is to remain great, its
public servants must overcome this provincialism. What they
propose for London must be capable of universal application: it should become a pattern for every other urban community, for every other region in Britain. Thus London,

instead of further weighing down the whole Commonwealth with its burdens, would set a pattern for what in time would become a world-wide renewal of civilization. In that act, the great qualities London has shown in war would be carried over into the peace.

7. PRECONDITIONS OF URBAN RE-BUILDING

What is the most essential fact that must be recognized in the re-planning of London and every other great area in Britain? The most essential fact is that which the Plan of London lightly sets to one side: the fact that we have reached a critical phase in our civilization, in which every effort to continue living and building on past lines must lead to that final end-product, the Necropolis. If that be so, no little local measures will serve to restore life-processes. Before local improvement can be engineered, the broad outlines of new national policy must be established, and a new cycle of growth must be started.

In endeavoring to outline the most important aspects of a national policy that will further civic reconstruction I must raise many debatable issues without having the time or space to go adequately into their merits. Whatever use the following suggestions may have will be mainly in putting the discussion of urban re-building within a more adequate political and social frame.

The first governing consideration, it seems to me, is the framing of a positive national population policy. If the British people are not in the least concerned for their survival, the present Plan of London will perhaps serve to keep them brightly occupied for a few generations, until sterility and inanition cause them finally to disappear. Otherwise, the prime desideratum of town planning must be to provide an urban environment and an urban mode of life which will not be hostile to biological survival: rather to create one in which the processes of life and growth will be so normal to that existence, so visible, that by sympathetic magic it will encourage in women of the child-bearing age the impulse to bear and rear children, as an essential attribute of their humanness, quite as interesting in all its possibilities as the most glamorous success in an office or a factory.

Now, population growth will not come about solely from the better planning of cities: that goes without saying. The relations of urban size and density to the rates for fertility and survival are very complicated; for the apathy toward reproduction which during the last generation has resulted in a tapering off of vitality in the more "advanced" countries is the product, not of environmental factors by themselves, but environmental factors as the physical expression of a pervasive megalopolitan mode of life: a mode that has ceased to be life-centered and life-directed. Let us take an example: If a young couple have established themselves in a small apartment and have a single child, they may well be reluctant to have three or four children, when the addition of so many would involve, not merely a removal to poorer quarters, but a definite lowering of the whole level of life, as Alva Myrdal has demonstrated. Unless greater opportunities, greater interests, greater incentives can be offered to the child-bearing couple than to those who refuse parenthood, unless the former win social approval and social encouragement, child-bearing will remain unfashionable.

Now one of the first steps within the province of democratic political effort is to provide, for the mother confined to the home by her domestic duties, a domestic environment that is adequate to her needs. This means plenty of space within the house itself, so that a family of three or four children will not automatically become disorderly and distracting; it means an immediate play space for the younger children within sight of the mother at work, not eight stories below; it means opportunities for social meeting within her immediate neighborhood, with people of her own kind; it means the possibility for an active life of wife and husband together, also within the local community, through the provision of recreation grounds, public meeting rooms, opportunities for art and craft of all sorts; it means, for the continuity of the family itself, plenty of storage space for possessions and records; it means the provision of gardens for flowers, fresh greens, and even fruits, as a normal addition to the family income.

All these provisions demand a re-apportionment of the national income by either direct or indirect subsidies to families; but the most powerful form of support and encouragement to the acceptance of normal family responsibilities by all healthy parents—in contrast to the reckless encouragement of large families for the few—would be in the adequate provision of houses, gardens, and playing spaces. Here the standards that must be set down as a minimum demand low density and an open plan: somewhere between 36 and 84 per acre, depending upon the distribution of adults and the extent to which industry is combined with housing.*

Most present urban reconstruction, I must repeat, is based upon subsidizing the ground landlord whose putative values have been brought about by the blind over-massing of popu-

---

* One of the most questionable proposals in the L.C.C. plan is that for segregating London's characteristic small workshops into flatted buildings [English for lofts] instead of grouping them in an orderly fashion in low units closer to the domestic quarters, as with the factories in the older parts of Letchworth Garden City. Once overcrowding and muddle are done away with by open building there is much to be said for keeping the less noxious and noisy crafts within the residential neighborhood, for the sake of both convenience and education.

lation in limited urban areas. This explains why the provision of model tenements in London has steadily raised the density per acre, and now, in the latest plan, continues this process. A national population policy will have to make a radical, indeed a revolutionary, departure here: it will have to reduce the present structure of urban land values and create a new structure which will be more favorable to human reproduction.

But it is important to recognize that new babies will not probably be brought into the world, the way in which predatory animals are exterminated in some countries, merely by offering direct bounties per head. What is needed is a more general re-orientation of values, an increase of animal vitality and self-respect, a scheme of living which places love and parenthood at the very core of the community's activities. City-building must embody, in rational terms, the collective "life-wish." When the prospect of children is looked upon as "too, too sick-making," to use the horrible words of one of Evelyn Waugh's Bright Young Things of the thirties, the race, in every sense, is finished. Now, among university students in America, particularly among the girls, not least among the most able and promising ones, I have observed a radical change in attitude from their mothers' generation: babies and family life have become central again, and the attractions of a professional career, though not disdained, have become secondary. If that change has been taking place in England, it will set the stage for a positive population policy.

No country like Britain can afford a scheme of urban reconstruction which promises only to carry further its present tendencies toward sterility. If I am right, the distribution of houses and flats in the re-building schemes for the East End would be a positive population check. That kind of reconstruction, however bold in appearance, however satisfying in its esthetic order, would be fatal.

The second measure that is preliminary to the re-planning of London, therefore, is the deliberate alteration of the present structure of urban land values, not alone in London, but throughout Britain. Important steps toward this end have already been taken, beginning with the Town and Country Act of 1932, and carried further in principle by the more recent proposal in the Uthwatt report to ensure the state acquisition of development rights to prospective building land around cities. But these are only beginnings. To reduce the level of London's land costs to a point at which it would be possible to build family dwellings and balanced neighborhood communities, there must be a large-scale movement of population and industry from London to other centers, mainly new, or partly new, centers. This movement may conceivably be conducted in such a way as to serve a double economic purpose. First, by lessening the pressure on London's urban space it will, by quite normal economic processes, tend to lower land values there; and second, by the eventual rise in the economic rent of land in the new centers it may—provided the movement be conducted under a national authority—conserve the increment from the new centers and apply this toward relieving the burdens of compensation in London itself.

When I speak of compensation I mean only partial compensation: not alas! the "fair compensation" envisaged by the Uthwatt report. Frankly, I do not believe that urban England can be properly rebuilt within a reasonable time without the existing land owners' having to take a loss. On principles of "fair compensation" at the 1939 level, no national Exchequer could, at the end of a long, grueling war, also pay off its landlords on the scale needed for comprehensive urban reconstruction. The only question, then, is whether the change is to be fraudulently accomplished, as in Germany after the last war, by a ruinous wholesale inflation, or whether it is to be honestly managed on the principles of normal commercial bankruptcy, by persuading the creditors (the land owners) to take a fraction of the original land values. Nationalization of urban land on these latter terms seems to me the only alternative to permitting the present structure of land values to serve as a barrier to any effective planning and building. From the human standpoint, the great mass of England's urban communities are bankrupt: they share this fatal heritage with the rest of Western civilization. The sooner that impossible and insupportable debt is cleared off, the sooner will the processes of life be resumed.

This brings me to the third step preliminary to re-planning London. Along with the removal of large increments of population to new centers must go the removal of industry: town building and industrial re-settlement must be co-ordinated. That is the burden, of course, of the Barlow Committee's recommendations; and the Barlow Report is the most fundamental contribution to the planning movement that has yet been made by any public body. To reap the full benefits of industrial decentralization new cities must be founded, old ones must be reconstituted on a more open and organic pattern, and existing small centers must be rehabilitated and rounded out. In short, three different modes of planning will work to the same general result: balanced communities, limited in size, yet many-sided in their industrial and social activities, capable of making available to their citizens all the resources needed for a balanced life.

On this matter of industrial decentralization I have but two suggestions to make. The first is a minor one. With the experience the war has brought, why should it not be possible, in planning a large-scale emigration from London, to keep together at least part of the population of a borough or a group of related boroughs: to retain as much of their social identity as is possible in the new situation, moving pubs and publicans, no less than factories, schools and teachers no less than works managers and factory hands; one might even establish a continuity of name between, say, Stepney in the East End and "Stepney-in-the-Wold" or "Stepney-under-the-Hill." The city would be different, but the people, at first, would be the same, and the transition would be humanly a little easier than in the more random re-groupings of industry. The other suggestion is that the strategy of industrial decentralization should be the product of a central staff, directly responsible through its appropriate ministers to Parliament; but the actual carrying out of the program of industrial decentralization and urban re-centralization should be in the hands of an authority capable of dealing with every aspect of the problem, from the preservation of good rural land from urban encroachment to the actual planning of communities.

Hence the fourth and final precondition to re-planning London is one I have already touched on: the creation of a Regional Authority capable of acting over a much larger area than the London County Council, and of exercising an over-all control on the entire process of building. The division of Britain itself into regional administrative areas and the creation of a new pattern of decentralized government and administration, mid-way between national and municipal authorities, with closer knowledge of the region and closer affiliations to it than Whitehall can presume to have, and yet armed with the authority and power to consider every local measure in its relation to broad national policy, seems to me

an essential political step toward any particular city's reconstruction.

Here again, the admirable political inventiveness which
originally created the great Port of London Authority need
only to follow its own bold precedents to provide both individual industries and individual municipal and county authorities with the very implements they need if they are to
carry out measures which exceed, in their scope and intention, the limits of their own natural capacities. Even the
county of London, as I have tried to show, is as limited as
its most feeble borough in trying to deal single-handed with
the tasks it confronts for its own rehabilitation. As the scale
of communication and co-operation has increased, such Regional Authorities have become as essential to local government as the municipality itself was a hundred years ago.

Let me sum up. The preconditions for the re-planning of
London are: 1. a National Population Policy, looking toward
its stabilization, if not its increase, instead of permitting the
threatened decrease of population to go on unchecked. 2. A
Policy of Urban Land Nationalization which will liquidate
the present structure of urban values and permit large-scale
reconstruction to be economically carried on, in a fashion
favorable to family life and balanced communal relationships. 3. A National Policy of Industrial Decentralization
along the lines laid down in the Barlow Report: a policy
which will progressively move population out of London and
other large centers until a net reproduction rate close to 1.0
is achieved. 4. Regional administrative units that will undertake the task of re-settlement and building outside the existing
municipal or county areas and will co-ordinate the work of
the municipalities themselves.

Planning in other words is a twofold process: one part of
it is national in scope and rests upon the formulation of na-

tional policies; the other part is regional and local. Ideally the two should converge toward a common point. Urban plans that are now being framed in a more or less independent fashion, even when the work is conceived by the puissant London County Council, will, in the very act of being practical and keeping their nose to the ground, serve the country ill. The most practical plans that can now be conceived are those ideal schemes which cope with the realities of survival and renewal, schemes which depart from the blind tendencies that prevailed before the present catastrophe and that do not hesitate to pay the price for renewal, knowing that no price is too high for life itself, if it be an honorable bargain.

Urban planning today is nothing if it does not plan for leaving behind the doomed Necropolis, or rather, for saving it from doom by opposing all the processes that stifled man there and by opening up a fresh field for life and work even within the old metropolitan areas themselves. To build intelligently today is to lay the foundations for a new civilization. The working out of that change will be a long process: not done in a day, not perhaps in a century. But the first steps toward reconstruction, to be effective, must point clearly to that end.

INDEX

NOTE—Titles of books and other publications are printed in italics

Mechanical power, dream of, 158
Mechanisms, devitalized, 158
Mechanization, 163
Megalopolis, 37, 207, 211
Megalopolitan civilization, end products of, 208
Melville, Herman, 31, 41, 85, 125, 183
Men Must Act, 200
Metropolis, decentralization of, 185
Metropolis vs. Countryside, 218
Metropolises, overgrown, 161
Metropolitan civilization, failure of, 25
Metropolitan Economy, 186
Metropolitan land values, need to deflate, 171
Metropolitanism, defense of, 218; prospects of, 22; two kinds of, 23
Middle class housing, 65
Migration, Urban, in London, 223
Militarism, 163
Mill, John Stuart, 164
Moby-Dick, 31
Model flats, 226
Model T dilemma, 71
Modern apartments, 226
Modern house, communal dependence of, 79
Monopolies, 171
Moses, Robert, 115, 134, 139
Mother Waldron Playground, 127
Motherhood, preference for, 235
Motor cars, 159
Municipal Art Societies, 18
Municipal budgets, 108
Municipal deficits, 96
Museum, civic, 148
Museums, educational functions of civic, 148
Myrdal, Alva, 213, 233
Myrdal, Gunnar, 213

Nakedness, 124
Napoleon of Notting Hill, 203
National frontiers, 167
National income, re-apportionment of, 234
National population policy, 239
National Resources Committee, 101
Nationalization, need for urban land, 237

Nature, absence of in metropolis, 47
Nazism, poisons of, 165
Necropolis, 208, 220, 222, 232
Negations, financial and imperial, 44
Neighborhood, communal functions of, 193; house as part of, 80
Neighborhood playgrounds, 113; design of, 126
Neighborhoods, survey of, 115
Neo-Malthusianism, 199
Net reproduction rate, 213
New England town, 6
New York, 201; author's interpretation of, 26; dominance of, 23; 1811 plan for, 9; old, influence on author of, 26; portrait of, 28-60; probable fall of, 215; as traveler's city, 21; weather of, 39
New York State Housing and Regional Planning Commission, 70
Nolen, John, 83
Norman, Dorothy, 27
Nothing Gained by Overcrowding, 81
Nude Bathing, 124

Occupations, urban and rural, 184
Olmsted, Frederick Law, 6, 34, 115, 131
Open spaces, London's, 225, 228
Organisms, desocialized, 158
Organizations, fossilization of, 182
Osborn, F. J., 154
Our Cities, 101

Pacific Northwest, 85
Paper, Cult of, 32
Parasitopolis, 37, 222
Parent, role of, 181
Park, aquatic, 124
Park girdle, 98
Park development, 99
Park planning, as key to urban development, 130
Park policies, 99
Parkchester project, 171
Parks, congestion in, 131; people's, 132; counsel of economy for, 133
Parkways, function of, 119; military importance of, 120
Patholopolis, 37
Peabody, George, 226